OXFORD ENGLISH MEMOIRS AND TRAVELS

General Editor: James Kinsley

The Life of Edward, First Lord Herbert of Cherbury

The
Life of Edward,
First Lord Herbert
of Cherbury

written by himself

Edited with an Introduction by
J. M. Shuttleworth

LONDON
OXFORD UNIVERSITY PRESS
NEW YORK TORONTO
1976

Oxford University Press, Ely House, London W1.

GLASGOW NEW YORK TORONTO MELBOURNE WELLINGTON
CAPE TOWN IBADAN NAIROBI DAR ES SALAAM LUSAKA ADDIS ABABA
DELHI BOMBAY CALCUTTA MADRAS KARACHI KUALA LUMPUR
SINGAPORE JAKARTA HONG KONG TOKYO

Introduction, Notes, Bibliography, Chronology, and Index
© Oxford University Press 1976

British Library Cataloguing in Publication Data

Herbert, Edward, Baron Herbert, b. 1581/2
    The life of Edward, first Lord Herbert
    of Cherbury. – (Oxford English memoirs
    and travels).
    Bibl. – Index.
    ISBN 0–19–255411–5
    1. Shuttleworth, J M 2. Series
    192   B1201.H34
    Herbert, Edward, Baron Herbert, b. 1581/2

Printed in Great Britain
by W & J Mackay Limited, Chatham

Contents

Illustrations

Acknowledgments

In the ten years since I first began a study of Lord Herbert's *Life*, I have incurred many academic debts and benefited from many scholarly kindnesses. I happily acknowledge them here: the Earl of Powis and Mr. David Jenkins of the National Library of Wales, for kind permission to use the Herbert manuscripts; the manuscript staffs of the National Library of Wales and of the British Library, both unfailingly helpful; Professors Gerald Chapman and Gunnar Boklund of the University of Denver, for travel grants and sound guidance; Colonel Jesse Gatlin, Department of English and Fine Arts, United States Air Force Academy, who encouraged my undertaking; Mrs. Betty H. Fogler, USAF Academy Library, who imaginatively and tenaciously found research materials not normally available in Colorado; my colleagues, Professors William Dwyer and James Grimshaw, for patient help in proofreading several drafts; the Revd. Mr. Michael Peel, formerly Vicar of Cherbury, now Rector of Iver Heath, and Mrs. Peel, for generous hospitality and gracious counsel; Miss Anne Charvet, Oxford University Press, whose editorial advice and diligence are exceeded only by her patience in seeing this transatlantic project come to fruition; and, of course, my wife Barbara, whose forbearance and encouragement are limitless.

If flaws remain despite the generosity of those named here, they are mine alone.

J.M.S.
United States Air Force Academy
25 August 1975   Colorado

vii

Introduction

EDWARD HERBERT's *Life* has delighted and instructed its readers for more than three hundred years. Its enduring charm lies in the conscious and unconscious self-revelation made by its author, one of those widely skilled men who took all knowledge for his province and whose accomplishments in many endeavours merit our admiration. To students of literature he is known as a poet and brother of the more famous George Herbert, the son of Magdalen Herbert (later Lady Danvers), Donne's friend, and the friend of Ben Jonson, Thomas Carew, Thomas Hobbes, and John Selden. To students of philosophy he is known as Herbert of Cherbury, father of English deism. The historian knows him as King James's ambassador to the French court (1619–24) and as the author of a standard history, *The Life and Raigne of King-Henry the Eighth* (1649).

His most revealing work, the *Life*, is today little known and less read. Yet he reveals in the autobiography and his other writings nearly all the forces that were striving for dominance in the early seventeenth century. He stands apart from the Puritan and Anglican controversies, but embraces elements of both in his philosophy. He seems to have been little affected by Bacon's *Novum Organum* in his autobiography, but in his *Henry VIII*, modelled on Bacon's *Henry VII*, he went to original sources to reach impartial truth rather than be bound by tradition. In his English prose writings he generally adopted the plain, direct style, yet his philosophical works and some of his poetry were written in turgid Renaissance Latin. In his philosophy he tended toward realism rather than materialism, yet he emphasized the *thing* as the stimulus of man's ideas. He embraced elements of

Aristotle and Plato, Aquinas and Scotus, Stoicism and neo-Platonism in a philosophical eclecticism which mirrors the confusion of the age. An aristocrat, he served the king and kingdom loyally as an ambassador; but in his poetry he attacked monarchy and the state as evil.[1] He devoted much of his life to the study of philosophy, yet in the autobiography he says that one year is 'enough for Philosophy as I conceiue and six moneths for Logick for I am Confident a man may haue quickly more than hee needes of those two arts'. Although he declared himself a man of peace, he nevertheless engaged in several quarrels. He was, in sum, as self-contradictory as the political and intellectual age in which he lived: a gentleman adventurer and dilettante philosopher, the last knight-errant and the first deist.

To understand why only a few hints of the deistic philosopher appear in the autobiography—almost shyly introduced as if they did not quite belong in the fun-loving, quick-witted, courtly character he created—one must go beyond the autobiography to Herbert's life, his ambition, his philosophy, and the circumstances in which he began but never completed this 'notice to his posterity'.

Herbert was born in his maternal grandmother's house at Eyton-on-Severn, Shropshire, between twelve and one o'clock in the afternoon of 3 March 1581/2.[2] His family on both sides were wealthy landed gentry, the foremost families in the Welsh–English border country. Herbert's early childhood, marred by illness, was probably an uneventful one somewhat dominated by his famous mother, Magdalen. On 14 May 1596, at the age of fourteen, he was enrolled as a gentleman-commoner of University College, Oxford. He was early given to speculation, if his autobiography can be believed, and he continued in this habit at Oxford. In October of that year he was called home at his father's death and thereafter became the ward of Sir George More, later Donne's unwilling father-in-law. The young

---

[1] 'The State-Progress of Ill', in *Poems English and Latin*, ed. G. C. Moore Smith (1923; 1968), pp. 9–13.

[2] For the date of Herbert's birth see M. M. Rossi, *La Vita, Le Opere . . . Chirbury* (Florence, 1947), iii. 376–8, hereafter cited as *La Vita*. Also see Rossi's note in *Modern Language Notes*, lxiii (1948), 144.

Herbert wrote with affection to Sir George, who seems to have taken a kindly interest in his ward.

Two years later, when he was sixteen, he was married to his cousin Mary, daughter of Sir William Herbert of St. Julians, five years Edward's senior and heiress to her father's estates in England, Wales, and Ireland.[3] The marriage was not a grandly romantic one, but it seems to have been a sound one with loyalty and consideration on both sides, despite the presence and probable supervision of his mother during the young couple's residence at Oxford.[4]

After some ten years of marriage Herbert, stirred perhaps by his youthful experiences at court and by induction into the Order of the Bath, both of which he relates with much relish, desired to see the world and make a name for himself as a gentleman-adventurer. For ten years more he was often abroad enjoying the adventures he vividly narrates in the autobiography. We may suspect that his friendships with the Prince of Orange and the English leaders in the Low Countries and with the Elector and Electress Palatine during those years did much to stimulate his ambition.

After Buckingham urged his appointment as ambassador to France in 1619, his fortune seemed assured; but like his brother George, Sir Edward Herbert was doomed after his brief moment of glory to a similar, even a more bitter disappointment than that which his brother suffered. The world of bright promise, advancement, and wealth which lay before him when Buckingham had nominated him clouded to dismal and vain hope after his abrupt recall. In the summer of 1624 Herbert returned from France disappointed, frustrated of his courtly ambition, and sorely in debt.[5] On 30 December 1624 he was rewarded with the cheapest of tokens, being made Lord Herbert of Castle Island in the Irish peerage, a title derived from his wife's

[3] See W. H. Smith, ed., *Herbert Correspondence* (Cardiff, 1963) and James Hanford, 'Lord Herbert . . . and his Son', *Huntington Library Quarterly*, v (1941), 317-32, for the long conflict this land ultimately wrought between Lord Herbert and his son Richard.

[4] Lady Herbert established her London house, after leaving Oxford, in April 1601.

[5] Rossi, *La Vita*, ii. 371ff., prints a full account of Herbert's recall.

estates in County Kerry. The failure of King James and later of Charles to recognize Herbert's not inconsiderable achievements— or at least to compensate him for the heavy indebtedness incurred in their service—must weigh heavily when with hindsight we judge his vacillation during the Civil War.

For the next fifteen years he continued to seek royal favour. He petitioned Charles I on 8 May 1626 for the English baronetcy promised him by the new king's father and for a seat on the Privy Council. Neither was granted, nor was the £3,000 recompense he sought.[6] In another move to remain in favour he attempted to justify Buckingham's disastrous leadership of the expedition against the French on the Island of Rhé, but his loyalty to Buckingham could not overcome his sense of truth, for he allows himself on occasion to indict the murdered favourite.[7]

On 7 May 1629 he was finally made Baron Herbert of Cherbury,[8] and in June 1632 he took his place on the king's Council of War as a member of the committee for drawing up 'fit instructions for all persons in command of garrisons and forts'.[9] In 1632 he began one last attempt to win favour with what was to become an exhaustive history of Henry VIII modelled on Bacon's earlier treatment of Henry VII (1622). For seven years he laboured intermittently on this work which was finally published in 1649, after his death. In his research he was assisted by Thomas Masters, who returned to Oxford in 1639 when it was complete. But the events taking place in the political life of the country prevented either reward or recognition for his labour. He was summoned with the other nobility to York in 1639 when the king levied an army against the Scots, but he returned

[6] The letter is printed in *Notes and Queries*, 4th series, x. 222, and Lee's edition of the autobiography, p. 139.

[7] *The Expedition to the Isle of Rhé* (1656; 1860) was written in 1629 and 1630. A copy Herbert presented to King Charles is now in the National Library of Wales.

[8] Because the title of Montgomery had been pre-empted by his cousin, Philip Herbert, in 1605, Lord Herbert took his title from the Shropshire manor and village of Chirbury three miles east of Montgomery Castle.

[9] *Calendar of State Papers, Domestic*, v. 364. (Hereafter *Cal. S.P.*)

to Montgomery shortly after the futile expedition.[10] From 1640 until May of 1642, as his health would permit, Herbert took a desultory part in the affairs of the House of Lords. He served on several minor committees and urged moderation when he spoke. On one occasion when the Lords were in debate over sending to the king a petition that declared all those who assisted him in warring against the Parliament to be traitors Herbert spoke against the affront, saying, 'I should agree to it, if I could be satisfied that the King would make War upon the Parliament without Cause'. For speaking out he was remanded to the custody of the Gentleman Usher, but was the next day released.[11]

Thereafter, he retired to Montgomery, unable because of bad health and disinclination to support the royal house which had treated him so shabbily, and in disagreement with the increasing extremism of Parliament. His castle was threatened by Royalists in 1644 and Herbert admitted a Parliamentary garrison under Sir Thomas Myddleton on 5 September 1644. He removed to London, living in his house in Queen Street near St. Giles's, where he returned to the study of philosophy that he had pursued throughout his life. He finished two philosophical works, *De Religione Laici* and *De Causis Errorum*, to supplement his earlier *De Veritate* (1624); and worked when health would permit on the autobiography begun the preceding year.

In counterpoise to the superficial frivolity of much of the autobiography were Herbert's real accomplishments in philosophy. More than his historical writings, his poetry, or his loyal service as an ambassador, his philosophical works give him a solid claim to a position of importance in the development of philosophy. The most famous (or notorious) parts of Herbert's philosophy were his five common notions of religion, to which he alludes in the autobiography (pp. 30–31). He believed that religion was common to

[10] The account of Lord Herbert's expenses in the journey north with his brother, Henry, is included in Add. MS. 37357, folios 26–7. The two Herberts took eight days from Ribbisford to York, arriving 15 April 1639.

[11] *Journal of the House of Lords*, 20 and 21 May 1642.

all men; that stripped of all priestly accretions it can be reduced to five innate ideas: (1) that there is a God; (2) that He is to be worshipped; (3) that virtue and piety are essential to worship; (4) that man should repent of his sins; (5) that there are rewards and punishments after this life.

By innate ideas Lord Herbert meant not that an infant is born with these beliefs, but that a normal person who attains his growth and reasons naturally is bound to come to them. An outgrowth of the five notions is an insistence on universal assent as the hallmark of truth; truth exists and is universal, eternal, and self-evident to all men. All men using right reason may attain to it. Because universal assent is the mark of truth man cannot be expected to accept a religion requiring implicit faith; and religion which claims general validity must justify itself on rational grounds, rather than ask its followers to accept the validity of revelation to another person. The man who does have a divine revelation—Lord Herbert did not deny revelation, as his conclusion of the *Life* will witness—must have prepared for the revelation; he must be made conscious of it in a distinct way; and must be motivated by it to do good. The implications of this belief are obviously far-reaching, for it amounts to saying that the independent conscience is supreme and not to be fettered by external authority, that no revealed truth can have validity except in the perception of the person to whom it occurs. All purely formal, traditionalist religion is thus dismissed at a sweep in the drive for individual awareness of truth.[12]

Truth, to which man assents by nature, is of four classes: (1) *veritas rei*, the truth of the object itself; (2) *veritas apparentiae*, factors external to the object, which relate to the way it appears; (3) *veritas*

[12] Although he is reported to have had prayers said daily in his house, the extent of Herbert's unconcern for formal religion is apparent in the story of his death on 20 August 1648. Aubrey relates that (James) 'Ussher, Lord Primate of Ireland, was sent for by him, when on his deathbed, and he would have received the sacrament. He sayd indifferently of it that "if there was good in any-thing 'twas in that" or "if it did not good 'twould doe no hurt". The primate refused it, for which many blamed him'. (*Brief Lives*, ed. Andrew Clark, i. 307.) At his request Lord Herbert was buried at midnight without ceremony in the yard of St. Giles-in-the-Fields.

conceptus, the truth as it is apprehended within man; (4) *veritas in-tellectus*, the truth of the intellect, the highest truth within man which judges presented truth by means of innate intelligence. The truth of intellect is placed in man's mind by God where it remains latent until stimulated by sensory perceptions, when it then determines the validity of those sensory perceptions.

Corresponding to the classes of truth are the four faculties of the mind. They are: (1) Internal Sense (conscience), which distinguishes the agreeable from the disagreeable, good from evil; (2) External Sense, what is commonly known as sensation; (3) Discursive Faculty, or reason, which deals with the knowledge purveyed by the senses; (4) Natural Instinct, present in the other three, is the source of the common notions, truths, and principles which exist in every human being.

The natural instinct is the source of the common notions in so far as it is the repository in which they remain until stimulated by ex-ternal things perceived through the senses. The common notions, however, come directly from God and are implanted within us by Him and are His imprint; they are independent of man's conscious reason. The objective peculiar to this natural instinct is personal happiness; it is both the inspiration and instrument of man's search for happiness. Natural instinct bears the same relation to the other faculties or instincts as the natural law does to laws. Since man is naturally led to good and since every good leads to a better one, the last of the series must be the sovereign good, which is logically identified with the object of the natural instinct.[13]

The reaction to Herbert's philosophy, which came largely in the century following his death, took two forms: violent attack or earnest support. But the reader of the *Life* will find nothing of the reactions and little philosophical influence, except perhaps in Her-bert's occasional concern for physical detail. A philosophy which holds that the reality of sense leads to truth might incline Herbert to

[13] Herbert's often confused and obscure philosophy is discussed in Carre's edition of *De Veritate*, an article by H. G. Wright in *Modern Language Review*, xxviii (1933), 295-307, and in R. H. Popkin's *The History of Scepticism* (1964), 155-74.

be concerned with colour, texture, taste, location, and attitudes, but the extent to which we owe the descriptive detail of the *Life* to his philosophy is a matter for speculation.

In earlier years, Herbert has been charged with an over-active Welsh imagination or with attempting to recapture a lost youth in a lonely old age, either of which led him to exaggerate and fabricate out of whole cloth much of his autobiography. While there may be something in either of those charges, Rossi has demonstrated exhaustively the essential truthfulness of the autobiography. Although Lord Herbert on occasion may unconsciously deceive himself about his reception, his life-long philosophical concern with the nature of truth led him to a largely factual history of himself, a not insignificant achievement when we realize the circumstances in which he wrote.

He was past sixty, he tells us, when he began his memoirs. What he neglects to say is that for several years he had been ill and was twice granted leave from the House of Lords.[14] His ill health was made worse by his loneliness; his wife had died in 1636; he was increasingly alienated from his royalist sons; all his brothers except Sir Henry had died before 1640. In June 1643, during the time he was composing the autobiography, he wrote to Sir Henry: 'I am thinkinge of a journey to the Spaw; but I doubt how I shal be able to go, my body being more infirme then to endure any labour. And let me assure you, I finde myselfe grown older in this one yeare than in fifty-nine yeares before; . . . And here I must remember that of all of us, there remains now but you and I to brother it.'[15]

Yet, in his autobiography we see none of his suffering or loneliness, no self-pity. Instead, the character he reveals is that of an indomitable, vigorous, and successful youth, living life fully and sometimes foolishly, relishing the marks of favour and the grati-

[14] See *La Vita*, iii. 191-370. He was first granted leave to absent himself on 21 May 1642 and it was renewed on 24 October 1644 (*Journal of the House of Lords*, v. 77; vii. 32). He speaks of 'defects of sight and hearing' in petitions to Parliament in 1646 (*Correspondence*, nos. 186, 187).

[15] 14 June 1643. The letter is printed in *Montgomeryshire Collections*, vi. 421, and in *La Vita*, iii. 192n.

fication of an abundant ego. The knight-errant had, for the hours of composition, imprisoned the first of the deists.

Horace Walpole, Herbert's first editor and a largely unsympathetic one, provided in the 'Advertisement' to his edition a still apt summary of Lord Herbert's life:

As a public Minister, he supported the dignity of his country, even when its Prince disgraced it; . . . These busy scenes were blended with, and terminated by meditation and philosophic inquiries. Strip each period of its excesses and errors, and it will not be easy to trace out, or dispose the life of a man of quality with a succession of employments which wou'd better become him. Valour and military activity in youth; business of state in middle age; contemplation and labours for the information of posterity in the calmer scenes of closing life: This was Lord Herbert.

Note on the Text

THIS TEXT is based on the original manuscripts of Lord Herbert's *Life* now deposited in the National Library of Wales under the general heading of Powis MSS. The *Life* exists in two forms: a manuscript in a seventeenth-century hand with corrections by Lord Herbert and a derivative manuscript in a nearly modern hand. Because the first MS. is incomplete both MSS. provide readings for this edition.

AuE

The earlier MS. is designated *AuE* by Rossi to indicate the version of the autobiography (*Au*) in the hand of Rowland Evans (*E*), Lord Herbert's secretary (1639–*c*. 1645) at the time it was composed.[1] I follow Rossi's designations. Evans, who received his education at Hart Hall, Oxford (B.A., 1622/3), was not a professional scribe: his orthography is too variable, his script too irregular. Evans writes in the secretary's hand of the late sixteenth century using conventional scribal contractions. Except for the occasional passages which were hurriedly written or heavily corrected, the script is reasonably clear.[2] Despite its being written in Evans's hand, the authenticity of *AuE* is proven beyond doubt by the corrections Lord Herbert made throughout the MS. Herbert's script, wherever it appears, is laboured, crabbed, and heavy, probably the result of an arthritic attack in

[1] *La Vita*, iii, Appendix xxxi.
[2] The MS. has forty-eight leaves containing pages 13-28, 33-72, 85-100, 105-20, 137-44.

1643 or 1644. From the nature of the errors and their corrections, made at various times over several months, it is clear that large portions of the MS. were dictated to Evans—whether from an earlier MS. in Herbert's hand or from *ex tempore* composition is, of course, impossible to determine now with certainty. Other portions of the MS. were just as clearly transcribed from an earlier version. The errors of transcription and the errors of dictation fall into a discernible pattern which allows us to see generally which parts of the MS. were dictated and which were transcribed. The gaps in the numbers below represent both the pages missing from the MS. and the pages on which neither sort of error occurred:

Errors of Dictation	*Errors of Transcription*
13–28	34–8
39–46	49–56
57–72	93–100
85–91	105–7
108–15	119–44

That errors of transcription should occur points to the existence of an earlier copy; that the periods of transcription are interspersed among periods of dictation further suggests that Herbert was reading from the earlier copy and altering as he read. If this is so we might also expect him to alter significantly those passages which Evans transcribed from the earlier version, as indeed he does in one cluster at *AuE* 93–9 (pp. 64–70 *infra*) where appears the greatest single grouping of Herbert's written corrections. They occur in a passage which is free from dictation changes and which has two transcription errors.

The corrections in Herbert's hand were made almost contemporaneously with the writing of the MS., for they nearly all appear in *AuW*, the second of the two extant MSS. Two series of corrections in Evans's hand, however, do not appear in *AuW* which instead repeats the uncorrected version of *AuE*. Therefore, those corrections are later additions, made after *AuW*'s source was copied. Since *AuW* contains a 1645 version of the Latin poem 'Vita', we may assume its source, a hypothetical *AuX*, was copied from *AuE* late in 1644 or early in 1645. Shortly thereafter and before he left Lord Herbert's employ, Rowland Evans made additional corrections at the author's command.

AuW

The existence of an intermediate MS. becomes certain when one compares *AuW* with the earlier *AuE*. Unlike *AuE*, this MS. is written with very few corrections in a neatly uniform, nearly modern script and orthography. Its later date is firmly established by its paper, for it bears watermarks which date from about 1698 to 1729.[3] *AuW* is the MS. Horace Walpole used in setting his type for the first printed edition (*Au1764*). Not only do we have Walpole's own testimony,[4]

[3] Edward Heawood, *Watermarks mainly of the 17th and 18th Centuries* (Hilversum, 1950), nos. 455 and 461. *AuE*'s watermarks most closely resemble Heawood's number 2097, dating from 1620 to 1640.

[4] Walpole writes in the 'Advertisement' to the first edition: 'The MS. was in great danger of being lost to the World. Henry Lord Herbert, grandson of the Author, died in 1691 without issue, and by his will left his Estate to Francis Herbert of Oakly-park, (father of the present Earl of Powis) his sister's son. At Lymore in Montgomeryshire (the chief Seat of the Family after Cromwell had demolished Montgomery Castle) was preserved the original Manuscript. Upon the marriage of Henry Lord Herbert with a daughter of Francis Earl of Bradford, Lymore, with a considerable part of the Estate thereabouts, was allotted for her jointure. After his decease, Lady Herbert usually resided there; she died in 1714. The MS. could not then be found: yet while she lived there, it was known to have been in her hands. Some years afterwards it was discovered at Lymore among some old papers, in very bad condition [I presume this is *AuE*], several leaves being torn out and others stained to such a degree as to make it scarcely legible. Under these circumstances, inquiry was made of the Herberts of Ribbisford (descended from Sir Henry Herbert a younger brother of the author-lord) in relation to a duplicate of the Memoirs, which was confidently said to be in their custody. It was allowed that such a duplicate had existed but no one cou'd recollect what was become of it. At last, about the year 1737, this book was sent to the Earl of Powis by a Gentleman, whose father had purchased an Estate of Henry Herbert of Ribbisford (son of Sir Henry Herbert above mentioned) in whom was revived in 1694 the title of Chirbury, which had extinguished in 1691. By him (after the sale of the Estate) some few books, pictures and other things were left in the house, and remained there to 1737. This Manuscript was amongst them; which not only by the contents (as far as it was possible to collate it with the original) but by the similitude of the Writing, appeared to be the Duplicate, so much sought after.'

I assume that the second complete copy Walpole describes is *AuW* in spite of his claim of similarity between the two very different scripts. See *La Vita*, iii. 512.

but we have considerable textual evidence. *AuW* and *Au1764* agree, with only minor variants, in substantive readings; both omit three passages present in *AuE*. Throughout the MS. appear non-authorial alterations in three hands, all but one of which are printed in *Au1764*, but none of which appears in *AuE*. The three passages bowdlerized from *AuW* by the copyist concern indiscretions of Herbert's cousin, Herbert's five 'Catholique Articles', and the Gunpowder Plot. These passages are restored to the complete text for the first time in this edition.[5]

That *AuW* was copied from an intermediate MS. is clear. Because of the date of the paper it could not have been made during Herbert's lifetime. If it had been made directly from *AuE* after Herbert's death the copyist would surely have followed all the corrections in Herbert's and Evans's hands instead of taking some readings which are heavily deleted in *AuE*. Likewise, he would have taken the final state of the Latin poem rather than an intermediate state. Walpole himself indicates corroborating evidence of an *AuX* when he speaks of a third MS. besides the two he knew. To a note in his own copy of the fourth edition (1770) of the *Life* which supplies the missing passage about Herbert's cousin, he adds that 'this paper was given to me in 1789, by W. Seward, Esq., who told me it was copied by Mr. Ingram from the original MS., which MS., I suppose is the copy of the Memoires of which I had heard, but never saw. The passage was not in the copy which Lord Powis lent me, and from which this edition was printed.'[6] Since the complete passage appears in *AuE* we must assume that Walpole did not carefully collate the incomplete and badly written MS. with the seemingly complete and clean copy of *AuW*. Thus, the Ingram MS. may well have been the *AuX* or a descendant collateral with *AuW*.[7]

[5] pp. 43, 29–31, and 39–40 *infra*. These passages were first printed by R. I. Aaron in *Modern Language Review*, xxxvi (1941), 184–94.

[6] Horace Walpole, *Letters*, ed. Peter Cunningham (1877), iv. 275.

[7] This theory, Rossi established, would account for Sir Henry Herbert's willingness to give a copy (*AuE*) to Lord Powis; he had in his possession one he could consider an original, *AuX*. The possibility of its being descended from *AuX* rather than being *AuX* itself is a distinct one, for in an age of increased antiquarian interest

Without the presence of an *AuX* these two MSS., *AuE* and *AuW*, are the only sources for any of the printed editions of the *Life*. In this edition *AuE* is the basic copy-text, for it is clearly the earlier, dictated and corrected by Lord Herbert. *AuW*, demonstrably later, occasionally corrupt, and bowdlerized, nevertheless must be resorted to for those passages missing from *AuE*, though we may not be reading Lord Herbert's precise words.

Treatment of the Text. The spelling of the copy-text has been followed exactly except in cases of contraction and obvious error, such as inadvertent or erroneous repetition or omission of a word or phrase. Contractions such as y^e, y^t, w^{th}, &, S^r, K^t, and contractions of proper names have been silently expanded. Passages in Latin or the other languages Lord Herbert uses have been neither expanded nor corrected.

A peculiar problem occurs in those passages where *AuW* is the only text available, *AuE* having been lost. *AuW* usually reads *wou'd*, *cou'd*, *'thô* for *AuE*'s invariable *would*, *could*, and *though*. In those instances I have silently expanded the contracted form to provide for greater consistency. I have not altered such spellings as *receiv'd* or *shew'd*, since AuE just as commonly has *receivd* as *received*, *shewd* as *shewed*.

I have not distinguished between long and short *s*, printing both as *s*. Double *f* is printed without notation as *F*. The old use of *u* and *v*, *i* and *j* is preserved except in the case of majuscule *J*. Whenever the pronoun *I* is intended or the initial letter of a word is an *I* it is so printed and no distinction is made between the two forms *I* and *J* which *AuE* uses interchangeably. In the use of capitals, I have other-

---

MSS. were often copied for friends. Some other references to MSS. are John Leland's *View of the Principal Deistical Writers* (1754), ii. 22ff., in which he prints the conclusion to the *Life* from a copy of the 'Memorials penn'd by (the author) himself', and Sloane MS. 4173, folios 5-20, by Thomas Birch. This is an extract of the autobiography which Birch says was copied in 1718 from an MS. in the possession of one Hone (Howe?) of Hanslope, Bucks. This copy is probably descended from *AuW*, for its spelling and punctuation are modern and it generally follows *AuW* in the forms of proper names.

wise followed the copy-text. The paragraphing is for the convenience of the modern reader; *AuE* has no clear paragraph breaks except at those points where work was interrupted, indicated in the MS. by partial lines and ink changes. In general I have followed the paragraphing of *Au1764*, the first version to indicate paragraphs. The punctuation is a compromise between seventeenth-century and modern practice. Evans's punctuation is hopelessly inconsistent and inadequate; the punctuation of *AuW*, while more modern and consistent, is not entirely reliable, suffers form a superfluity of commas, and has no clear textual authority. I have not noted emendation of punctuation except where it may substantially alter the meaning of a passage.

The significant variant readings will be found among the Textual Notes. They are based on a collation of the two basic MSS. and the two major editions, Walpole's printing of 1764 (*Au1764*) and Sir Sidney Lee's edition of 1906 (*AuLee*). They are limited to changes in word order, significant manuscript alterations, omissions, and additions. Since *AuLee* is derived from *Au1764* (not from manuscript, contrary to the editor's claim) and it in turn from *AuW*, the reader may assume that any variant listed for *AuW* was reprinted in *Au1764* and *AuLee* except where I have noted otherwise.

Select Bibliography

Editions of the LIFE. The first printed edition, Horace Walpole's *The Life of Edward Lord Herbert of Cherbury* (Strawberry Hill, 1764) has been the source for all subsequent versions until the present edition. Walpole's text, with varied appendices and annotations, was reprinted frequently: London, 1770, 1778, 1792, 1824, 1826; Dublin, 1771; Edinburgh, 1809 (with an introduction attributed to Sir Walter Scott). Other printings followed irregularly until Sir Sidney Lee's edition (London, 1886; rev. ed., 1906), especially useful for its attempts to identify every person Herbert names; its text, however, is corrupt. C. H. Herford wrote a perceptive introduction for the Gregynog Press edition (Newton, Mont., 1928).

Modern Editions of Herbert's Major Works. The Poems English and Latin, ed. G. C. Moore Smith (1923), has recently been reissued (1968). The poetry is also printed in R. G. Howarth's *Minor Poets of the Seventeenth Century* (1931; revised 1953). *De Veritate* was edited and translated by M. H. Carre (1937). H. R. Hutcheson edited and translated *De Religione Laici* (1944).

Studies. No complete bibliography yet exists for Herbert's writing, although both Rossi and Hutcheson include extensive listings. There is some treatment of the *Life* in Paget Toynbee (ed.), *Journal of the Printing Office at Strawberry Hill* (1923) and in A. T. Hazen's *Bibliography of the Strawberry Hill Press* (1942). The only comprehensive treatment of Herbert and his prose works appears in Mario M. Rossi, *La Vita, Le Opere e i Tempi de Eduardo, Lord Herbert di Chirbury,* 3 vols. (Florence, 1947). Rossi's earlier work *Alle Fonti del Deismo e*

del Materialismo Moderno (Florence, 1942) is also useful. Specialized
books and articles: Margaret Bottrall, *Every Man a Phoenix: Studies
in Seventeenth Century Autobiography* (1958); M. H. Carre's 'Review
of Rossi's *La Vita*' in *Mind*, lvii (1948), 237–44; R. W. Chapman,
'Lord Herbert . . . and the Bodleian', *Bodleian Quarterly Review*, vii,
174–5; D. H. Fordyce and T. M. Knox, 'The Library of Jesus College, Oxford with . . . the books . . . bequeathed . . . by Lord Herbert', *Proceedings and Papers of the Oxford Bibliographical Society*, v. 2
(1937), 53–115; Karl Güttler, *Lord Edward Herbert of Cherbury: ein
kritischer Beitrag zur Geschichte der Psychologimus und der Religions-
philosophie* (Munich, 1897); James J. Hanford, 'Lord Herbert of
Cherbury and His Son', *Huntington Library Quarterly*, v (1941),
317–32; J. W. Hebel, '*A Divine Love* addressed by Lord Herbert to
Lady Bedford', *Modern Language Review*, xv (1925), 74–6; for the
birthdate see D. A. Keister's 'The Birth Date of Lord Herbert of
Cherbury', *Modern Language Notes*, lxii (1947), 389–91 and Rossi's
correction in the same journal, lxiii (1948), 144; D. A. Keister,
'Donne and Herbert of Cherbury: an Exchange of Verses', *Modern
Language Quarterly*, vii (1947), 430–4; Keister also clarified Selden's
reference in 'Lady Kent and the Two Sir Edwards', *Modern Language
Notes*, lxi (1946), 169–72; Charles Lyttle, 'Lord Herbert of Cherbury,
Apostle of Ethical Theism', *Church History*, iv (December, 1935),
247–67; W. Moelwyn Merchant, 'Lord Herbert of Cherbury and
Seventeenth-Century Historical Writing', *Transactions of the
Honourable Society of Cymmrodorion*, Session 1956 (printed 1957),
47–63; Richard H. Popkin, *The History of Scepticism from Erasmus
to Descartes* (1964) has a chapter on Herbert's philosophy and reactions to it; C. F. M. Rémusat, *Herbert de Cherbury, sa vie et ses
oeuvres, ou les origines de la philosophie du sens commun et de la théologie
naturelle en Angleterre* (Paris, 1875); Frank J. Warnke, *This Metaphy-
sick Lord: A Study of the Poetry of Herbert of Cherbury* (Unpublished
dissertation; Columbia, 1954); Basil Willey's two essays 'Lord
Herbert of Cherbury: A Spiritual Quixote of the Seventeenth
Century', in *Essays and Studies of the English Association*, xxvii (1941),
11–19, and ch. 7 of *The Seventeenth Century Background* (1934).

A Chronology of
Edward, Lord Herbert of Cherbury

Chronology

The Life of Edward, Lord Herbert of Cherbury

I DO believe that if all my Ancestors had set down their Lives in writing, and left them to posterity, many documents necessary to be known of those who both participate of their natural inclinations and humours must in all probability run a not much different course, might have been given for their instruction; and certainly it will be found much better for Men to guide themselves by such observations as their Father, Grand-Father, and Great Grand-Father might have deliver'd to them, than by those vulgar Rules and Examples, which cannot in all points so exactly agree unto them. Therefore whether their Life were private, and contained only precepts necessary to treat with their Children, Servants, Tenants, Kinsmen, and Neighbours, or imployed abroad in the University, or Study of the Law, or in the Court, or in the Camp their Heirs might have benefited themselves more by them than by any else; for which reason I have thought fit to relate to my posterity those Passages of my Life, which I conceive may best declare me, and be most useful to them. In the delivery of which, I profess to write with all Truth and Sincerity, as scorning ever to deceive or speak false to any; And therefore detesting it much more where I am under obligation of speaking to those so near me, and if this be one Reason for taking my pen in hand at this time so as my Age is now past threescore, it will be fit to recollect my former actions, and examine what hath been done well or ill, to the intent I may both reform that which was amiss, and so make my peace with God, as also comfort my self in those things which through Gods great grace and favour, have been done according to the Rules of Conscience, Vertue and Honor. Before yet I bring my Self to this accompt, it will be necessary I say somewhat concerning my Ancestors. As far as the Notice of them is come to me in any credible way, of whom yet I cannot say much, since I was but eight years old when my Grand-Father died, and that my Father lived but about four years after; and that for the Rest I have lived for the most part from home. It is impossible I should have that intire knowledge of their Actions which might inform me sufficiently, I shall only therefore relate the more known and undoubted parts of their Lives.

My father was Richard Herbert, Esquire, Son to Edward Herbert, Esquire, and grandchild to Sir Richard Herbert, Knight, who was a younger son of Sir Richard Herbert of Colebrook in Monmouth-shire of all whom I shall say a little; and first of my Father; whom I remember to have been black haired and bearded as all my Ancestors of his side are said to have been, of a manly or somewhat stern look, but withall very handsome and well compact in his Limbs, and of a great courage, whereof he gave proof, when he was so barbarously assaulted by many Men in the churchyard at Lanervil[1] at what time he would have apprehended a man who denied to appear to justice, for defending himself against them all by the help only of one John ap Howell Corbet, he chaced his adversaries untill a Villain coming behind him did over the shoulders of others wound him on the head behind with a forest Bill[2] until he fell down, though recovering himself again, notwithstanding his skull was cutt through to the Pia Mater of the Brain, he saw his adversaries fly away, and after walked home to his house at Llyssyn,[3] where after he was cured, he offered a single Combat to the chief of the Family, by whose procurement it was thought the mischief was committed, but he disclaiming wholy the Action as not done by his consent, which he offered to testifie by Oath; and the Villian himself flying into Ireland, whence he never returned, My Father desisted from prosecuting the business any farther in that kind, and attained, notwithstanding the said hurt, that health and strength, that he returned to his former exercises in a country Life, and became the Father of many children. As for his Integrity in his places of Deputy Lieutenant of the County, Iustice of the Peace, and Custos Rotulorum which he as my Grand-Father before him held, it is so memorable to this day that it was sayd his enemies appeal'd to him for Iustice, which also they found on all occasions. His Learning was not vulgar, as understanding well the Latine Tongue, and being well versed in History.

My Grand-Father was of a various life beginning first at Court, where after he had spent most part of his Means, he became a Soldier, and made his Fortune with his Sword at the Siege of St. Quintens[1] in France, and other Wars, both in the North and in the Rebellions hapning in the times of King Edward the 6xt, and Queen Mary, with so good success, that He not only came off still with the better, but got so much money and wealth as enabled him to buy the greatest part of that livelyhood which is descended to me; though yet I hold some Lands which his Mother the Lady Ann Herbert purchased as appears by the Deeds made to Her by that name which I can show; and might have held more, which my Grand-Father sold under foot at an under value in his youth, and might have been recovered by my Father, had my Grand Father suffered him. My Grand-Father was noted to be a great enemy to the Outlaws and Thieves of his time, who robbed in great numbers in the Mountains in Montgomery-shire, for the suppressing of whom he went often both day and night to the places where they were, concerning which though many par-ticulars have been told me, I shall mention one only. Some Outlaws being lodged in an Alehouse upon the hills of Llandinam, my Grand-Father and a few servants coming to apprehend them, the Principal Outlaw shot an Arrow against my Grandfather which stuck in the Pummel of his Sadle, whereupon my Grandfather coming up to him with his sword in his hand, and taking him Prisoner, he showed him the said arrow, bidding him look what he had done, whereof the Outlaw was no farther sensible than to say he was sorry that he left his better bow at home which he conceiv'd would have carryed his shot to his Body, but the Outlaw being brought to Iustice, suffer'd for it. My Grand-Fathers power[2] was so great in the Countrey, that divers Ancestors of the better Families now in Montgomeryshire were his Servants, and raised by him. He delighted also much in Hospitality, as having a very long Table twice covered every Meal with the best Meats that could be gotten, and a very great Family.

3

It was an ordinary saying in the countrey at that time, when they saw any Fowl rise, fly where thou wilt, thou wilt light at Black Hall,[1] which was a low Building, but of great capacity, my Grand-Father erected in his Age; his Father and Himself in former times having lived in Montgomery Castle. Notwithstanding yet these expences at home, he brought up his Children well, married his Daughters to the better sort of Persons near him, And bringing up his younger Sons at the University; from whence his Son Matthew went to the Low Country Wars, and after some time spent there, came home, and lived in the countrey at Dolegeog[2] upon a house and fair living, which my Grand-Father bestowed upon him. His Son also Charles Herbert after he had past some time in the Low Countreys likewise returned home, and was after married to an Inheretrix,[3] whose Eldest Son Called Sir Edward Herbert, Knight, is the Kings Attorny Generall. His Son George who was of New Colledge in Oxford, was very learned, and of a pious life, died in a middle age of a Dropsy. Notwithstanding all which occasions of Expence, my Grandfather purchased much lands without doing any thing yet unjustly or hardly, as may be collected by an offer I have publickly made divers times, having given my Bailiffs in charge to proclaime to the Countrey, that if any Lands were gotten by evill means, or so much as hardly, they should be compounded for or restored again; but to this day, never any man yet complained to me in this kind. He died at the Age of fourscore or thereabouts, and was buried in Montgomery Church, without having any Monument made for him which yet for my Father is there set up in a fair manner.[4]

My Great Grand-father Sir Richard Herbert was Steward in the time of King Henry the Eight of the Lordships, and Marches of North-Wales, East-Wales, and Cardeganshire, and had power in a Marshal Law to execute Offenders; in the using thereof he was so just, that he acquired to himself a singular Reputation, as may appear upon the Records of that time, kept in the paper Chamber at White-Hall, some touch whereof I have made in my History of Henry the 8th; of him I can say little more than that he likewise was a great Suppressor of Rebells, Thievs, and Outlaws, and that he was just

In the third yeare of King James the Gunpowder
Treason happening My selfe who was Chosen Kt
of the Shire for Merionethshire at having
resigned my pretence in Mountgomeryshire to Sr
William Herbert at his entreaty did then Lodg in
my Mother house neare Charing Crosse, The
night before this horrible Conspiracy was to be
acted I was two severall tymes warned in my
sleepe not to goe to the Parliament that day
which though I tooke but for dreaming fell out
to bee an admonition; For Sr Walter Cope
comeing the 5th of November about six of the
Clocke told mee how the designe was discovered
wishing mee not to goe out of my house untill
things were better setled; Some few dayes
after the Lords of the Councill sent for mee
And because the Conspirators were now in a place
in Staffordshire not far from of Shropshire, they sent mee downe
with Commission to Levy forces to suppresse those who
were

and conscionable, for if a false or cruel person had that power committed to his hands, he would have rais'd a great Fortune out of it where of he left a litle, save what his Father gave him unto posterity. He lyeth buried likewise in Montgomery; the upper Monument of the two placed in the Chancell being erected for him.

My Great Great Grand-father Sir Richard Herbert of Colebrook was that incomparable Heroe (who in the History of Hall and Grafton[1]) as it appears, twice past through a Great Army of Northern men alone, with his Poll-ax[2] in his hand, and returned without any mortal hurt which is more than is famed of Amadis de Gall, or the Knight of the Sun.[3] I shall besides this Relation of Sir Richard Herbert's prowess in the Battle at Banbury or Edgcot-hill, being the place where the late Battle was fought, deliver some traditions concerning him, which I have receiv'd from good hands; one is, that the said Sir Richard Herbert being imployed together with his Brother William Earle of Pembrook to reduce certain Rebells in North-Wales, Sir Richard Herbert besciged a principal person of them at Harlech Castle in Merioneth shire; the Captain of this place had been a Soldier in the Wars of France, whereupon he said he had kept a Castle in France so long, that he made the old Women in Wales talk of him, and that he would keepe the castle so long that he would make the old Women in France talk of him, and indeed as the place was almost impregnable but by Famine, Sir Richard Herbert was constrained to take him in by composition, he surrend'ring himself upon condition, that Sir Richard Herbert should do what he could to save his Life, which being accepted, Sir Richard brought him to King Edward the 4th. desiring his Highness to give him a pardon, since he yeilded up a place of importance, which he might have kept longer upon this hope; But the king replying to Sir Richard Herbert, that he had no power by his Commission to pardon any, and therefore might after the Representation hereof to his Majesty, safe deliver him up to justice, Sir Richard Herbert answered he had not yet done the best he could for him and therefore most humbly desired his Highness to do one of two things, either to put him again in the Castle where he was, and command some other to take him out, or, if his Highness would not do so, to take his Life for the said Captain's, that being the last proof he could give that he used his uppermost endeavour to save the said Captain's life. The king finding himself urged thus far gave Sir Richard Herbert the life of the said Captain, but withall he bestowed no other reward for his service. The other History is that Sir Richard Herbert together with his Brother the Earle of Pembrook being in Anglesy apprehending there seven Brothers which had done many mischiefs and murders; in these times the Earle of Pembrook thinking it fit to root out so wicked a Progeny commanded them all to be hanged; whereupon the Mother of them coming to the Earle of Pembrook, upon her knees desired him to pardon two or at leastwise One of her said Sons, affirming that the Rest were sufficient to satisfie justice or example, which request also Sir Richard Herbert seconded; but the Earle finding them all equally guilty, said he could make no distinction betwixt them, and therefore commanded them to be executed together; at which the Mother was so aggreived, that with a pair of woollen Beads[1] on her arms (for so the Relation goeth) she on her knees curst him, praying God's mischief might fall to him in the first Batle he should make; The Earle after this, coming with his Brother to Edgcot field as is before set down, after he had put his Men in order to fight, found his brother Sir Richard Herbert in the head of his men, leaning upon his Poll-ax in a kind of sad or pensive manner, whereupon the Earle said, what doth thy great body (for he was higher by the head than any one in the Army) apprehend any thing that thou art so melancholy, or art thou weary with marching, that thou doest lean thus upon thy Poll-ax? Sir Richard Herbert replyed, that he was neither of Both, whereof he should see the proof presently: Only I cannot but apprehend on your part, least the curse of the Woman with the Woollen Beads fall upon you; This Sir Richard Herbert lyeth buried in Abergaveny in a sumptuous Monument[2] for those times, which still remains, whereas his brother the Earle of Pembrook being buried in Tintirne Abby, his Monument together with the Church lye now wholy defaced and ruind. This Earle of Pembrook had a younger Son which had a Daughter which married the eldest Son of the Earle of Worcester, who carried away the fair Castle of Ragland[1] with a many thousand pounds yearly from the Heir Male of that house, which was the second Son of the said Earle of Pembrook, and ancestor of the Family of St. Gillians, whose Daughter and Heir I after married, as shall be told in its place. And here it is very remarkable, that the younger Sons of the said Earle of Pembrook, and Sir Richard Herbert left their posterity after them who in the Person of my Self and my Wife united both houses again, which is the more memorable that when the said Earle of Pembrook and Sir Richard Herbert were taken prisoners in defending the just cause of Edward the fourth, at the Batle abovesaid, the Earle never intreated that his own life might be saved, but his Brothers, as it appears by the said History. So that joyning of both houses together in my posterity, ought to produce a perpetual obligation of friendship and mutual Love in them one to another, since by these two Brothers, so brave an example thereof was given, as seeming not to live or die but for one another.

My Mother was Magdalen Newport daughter of Sir Richard Newport and Margaret his Wife, daughter and Heir of Sir Thomas Bromley, one of the Privy Councell and Executor of King Henry the 8th. who surviving her husband gave rare testimonies of an incomparable Piety to God, and love to her Children, as being most assiduous and devout in her daily both private and publick prayers, and so carefull to provide for her Posterity; that though it were in her power to give her Estate (which was very great) to whom she would, yet she continued still unmaried and so provident for them, that after she had bestowed all her Daughters with sufficient portions upon very good neighbouring Families, she deliver'd up her Estate and care of housekeeping to her eldest Son Francis, when now she had for many years kept hospitality with that plenty and order as exceeded all either of her Countrey or time, for besides abundance of provision and good Cheer for Guests, which her Son Sir Francis Newport continued, she used ever after dinner to distribute with her own hands to the poor who resorted to her in great Numbers, Alms in Money, to every one of them more or less, as she thought they needed it; By these Ancestors I am descended of Talbot, Devoreux, Gray, Corbet, and many other Noble Families, as may be seen in their Matches, extant in the many fair Coats the Newports bear. I could say much more of my Ancestors of that side likewise, but that I should exceed my proposed scope: I shall therefore only say somewhat more of my Mother, my Brothers; and Sisters; and for my Mother, after she lived most vertuosly and lovingly with her husband for many years, she after his death erected a fair Monument for him in Montgomery Church, brought up her Children carefully, and put them in good courses for making their fortunes, and briefly was that Woman Dr Donne hath described in his funeral Sermon of her printed.[1] The names of her Children were, Edward, Richard, William, Charles, George, Henry, Thomas; her daughters were, Elizabeth, Margaret, Frances, of all whom, I will say a litle before I begin a Narration of my own Life, so I may pursue my intended purpose the more intirely. My Brother Richard after he had been brought up in Learning, went to the Low Countreys, where he continued many years with much Reputation both in the wars and for fighting single Duels, which were many, in so much that between both, he carried, as I have been told, the scars of four and twenty wounds upon him to his grave, and lyeth buried in Berghenapsoom:[2] My Brother William being brought up likewise in Learning went afterwards to the Wars in Denmark, where fighting a single combat, and having his sword broken, he not only defended himself, with that piece which remained, but closing with his adversary threw him down and so held him untill company came in; and then went to the Wars in the Low Countreys but lived not long after; My Brother Charles was Fellow of New College in Oxford, where he dyed young, after he had given great hopes of himself every way. My Brother George was so excellent a Scholar, that he was made the publick Orator of the University in Cambridge, some of Whose English Works are extant which though they be rare in their kind, yet are far short of expressing those perfections he had in the Greek and Latin Tongue, and all divine and human Literature: his Life was most holy and exemplary, in so much that about Salisbury where he lived beneficed for many years, he was litle less than Sainted: he was not exempt from passion and Choler, being infirmities to which all our Race is subject, but that excepted, without reproach in his Actions. Henry after he had been brought up in Learning as the other Brothers were, was sent by his Friends into France, where he attained the Language of that Country in much perfection, after which time he came to Court, and was made Gentleman of the Kings privy Chamber, and Master of the Revells, by which means as also by a good Marriage, he attained to great fortunes, for himself and Posterity to injoy: he also hath given several proofs of his Courage in Duells, and otherwise being no less dexterous in the Ways of the Court as having gotten much by it. My Brother Thomas was a Posthumus as being born some weeks after his Fathers death; he also being brought up a while at school, was sent as a Page to Sir Edward Cecil Lord Generall of his Majesties auxiliary forces to the Princes in Germany, and was particularly at the Siege of Juliers, Anno Domini 1610, where he shewed such forwardness, as no man in that great army before him was more adventurous on all occasions. Being returned from thence he went to the East Indias[1] under the command of Captain Joseph, who in his way thither, meeting with a great Spanish ship was unfortunately killed in fight with them, whereupon his Men being dishartned, my Brother Thomas encouraged them to revenge the Loss, and renewed the fight in that manner (as Sir Iohn Smyth Governour of the East India Company[2] told me at several times) that they forced the Spanish Ship to run a ground, where the English shot her through and through so often that she run her self a ground, and was left wholy unserviceable. After which tyme he with the rest of the Fleete came to Surratte And from thence went with the Marchants to the greate Mogull[3] where after he had stayd aboue a Tweluemoneth he returned with the same Fleete back againe to England.[4] After this time he went in the Navy[5] which king Iames sent to Argier vnder the Command of Sir Robert Mansell where our Men being in greate want of Money and Uictualls and many shipps scattering themselues to try whether they could obtayne a prize whereby to releive the wholle Fleete; It was his hap to meete with a Shipp which hee tooke and in it to the value of 1800 pound, which it was thought saued the wholle Fleete from perishing. He Conducted also Conte Mansfelt to the Lowe Countreys[1] in one of the Kings shipps which being vnfortunately cast away not farre from the shore The Conte (together with his Company) saued themselues in a long Boate or Shalop. The Benefitt whereof my said brother refused to take for the present as resoluing to assist the Master of the shipp who endeavoured by all means to cleare the shipp from the dannger, But finding it impossible he was the last man that saued himselfe in the long boate, The Master thereof yet refusing to come away so that he perished together with the shippe; After this hee commanded one of the shipps that were sent to bring the Prince from Spayne where vpon his returne there being a fight betweene the Lowe Countreymen and the Dunkirkiers The Prince, who thought it was not for his Dignity to suffer them to fight in his presence, commanded some of his shipps to part them wherevpon my said brother with some other shipps got betwixt them on either side and shott soe long That both partyes were glad to desist. After he had brought the Prince safely home, he was appointed to goe with one of the kings Shipps to the Narrow Seas;[2] He also fought diuers times with greate Courage and Successe with diuers men in Single fight sometimes hurting and disarming his Aduersary and sometimes driving him away. After all these Proofs giuen off himselfe he expected some greate Command, But finding himselfe (as he thought vndervalued, he retyred to a private and melancholly life, being much discontented to finde others preferred before him; In which sullaine Humor having lived many yeares, he dyed and was buried in London in St. Martins neare Charing Crosse, soe that of all my brothers none survives but Henry.

Elizabeth my Eldest sister was maried to Sir Henry Iones of Abermarles[3] who had by her one sonne and two daughters. The later end of her life was the most sickly and miserable that hath beene knowne in our tymes while for the space of 14 yeare she Languished and pinde away to skinne and bone and at last——dyed in London and lyeth buried in a Church called————neare Cheapside;

Margaret was married to Iohn Uaughan sonne and heire to Owen Uaughan of Llwydiart,[1] by which match some former differences betwixt our house and that were appeased and reconciled; He had by her three daughters and heires; Dorothy Magdalen and Katherine, Of which the two later onely survive; The estate of the Uaughans yet went to the heires males, though not soe clearely but that the Entayle which carried the sayd Lands was questioned. Frances my youngest Sister who was maried to Sir Iohn Brown Knight in Lincolneshire who had by her diuers children The Eldest sonne of whome (though young) fought diuers Duells, In one of which It was his Fortune to kill Lee[2] one of a greate Family in Lancashire; I could say many things more Concerning all these but it is not my purpose to particularize theire life. I haue related onely some passages concerning them to the best of my Memory, Being assured I haue not failed much in my Relation of them; I shall now come to my self.

I was borne at Eyton[3] in Shropshire, (being a house which together with faire Lands descended vpon the Newports by my said Grandmother) betweene the houres of twelve and one of the Clocke in the Afternoone; My Infancy was very sickly my hed continualy purging it selfe very much by the Eares, wherevpon also It was soe long before I began to speake That many thought I should bee euer dumbe. The very furthest thing I remember is, That when I vnderstood what was said by others I did yet forbeare to speake lest I should vtter something That were imperfect or impertinent. When I came to talke One of the first Inquiries I made was, How I came into this world; I tould my Nurse keeper and others I found my selfe here indeede but for what Cause or beginning or by what meanes I could not ymagine; But for this as I was laught at by my Nurse and some other women that were then present soe I was wondered at by others who said they neuer heard Childe but my selfe aske that Question; Vpon which when I came to riper yeares I made this Observation which afterwards a litle Comforted mee, that as I found my selfe in posession of this life without knowing any thing of the Pangs and throwes my Mother suffered when yet doubtlesse they did noe less presse and afflict mee then her, soe I hope my Soule shall passe to a better life then this without being sensible of the Anguish and paines my body shall feele in death, For as I beleiue then I shalbee transmitted to a more happy estate by Gods Greate Grace I am confident I shall noe more knowe how I came out of this worlde then how I came into it; And because since that tyme I haue made verses to this Purpose I haue thought fitt to insert them here as a place proper for them; The Argument is,

VITA[1]

Prima fuit quondam genitali semine Vita
Procurasse suas Dotes Vbi Plastica Virtus
Gestiet, et vegeto molem perfundere succo;
Externamq; suo formam cohibere recessu,
Dum conspirantes possint accedere Causae,
Et totum tuto licuit proludere foetum.
   Altera materno tandem succrevit in arvo
Exiles spumans vbi spiritus jnduit artus,
Exertusq; simul miro Sensoria textu
Cudit, et hospitium Menti non vile paravit,
Quae Caelo delapsa suas mox inde capessat
Partes, et sortis tanquam praesage futurae,
Corrigat ignavum pondus, nex jnutile sistat.
   Tertia nunc agitur, qua Scaena recluditur jngens,
Cernitur et festum Caeli Terraeq; Theatrum,
Congener et species, rerum variataq; forma;
Et circumferri, motu proprioq; vagari
Contigit, et leges aeternaq; faedera Mundi
Visere, et assiduo reduntia sydera cursu:
Vnde etiam vitae Causas nexumq; tueri.
Fas erat, et summum longe praesciscere Numen;
Dum varios mire motus contemperet Orbis
Et faciles aditus cui vis pia vota precesq;
Fundenti tribuit. Quid in modo QVARTA sequatur
Sordibus excussis cum mens jam purior instat,
Et nova successit melioris Conscia fati

Spes superis haerens toto lustrataq; Caelo.
Et sese sancto demittit Numen Amori;
Traditur aeterne hec fallax tessera Vitae,
Cumq; Deo licuit non uno jure pacisci.

And certainly since in my Mothers Wombe That Vis Plastica or
Formatrix which framed my Eyes, Eares and other senses, did not
intend them for that Dark and noysome place, but as being Conscious
of a better life made them as fitting Organes to apprehend and perceiue the things which should occure in this world, Soe I beleiue
since my coming into this world my soule hath formed or produced
certaine Facultyes, which are almost as vselesse for this life as the
abouenamed senses were for the Mothers wombe; and these Facultyes are Hope, Faith, Love, and Joy, Since they never rest or fix
vpon any Transitory or perishing Obiect in this world as extending
themselues to something further then can bec here given and indeed
acquiesce finally onely in the Perfect, Eternal and Infinite. I confesse
they are of some vse here yet I appeale to euery body whether any
worldly felicity did soe satisfy theire hope here That they did not
wish and hope for something more excellente or whether they had
euer that Faith in theire owne wisdome or in the help of man that
they were not constrained to haue recourse to some diuiner and
superior power then they could finde on earth to releiue them in
theire danger or Necessity, whether euer they could place theire
Love on any earthly beautye that did not fade and wither if not
frustrate and deceiue them Or whether euer theire Ioy was soe
Consummate in any thing they delighted in, That they did not want
much more then it or indeede this world can afford to make them
happy. The proper obiects of these Facultyes (though framed or at
least appearing in this worlde) is God onely vpon whome Faith,
Hope, and Love were never placed in vayne or long vnrequited, But
to leaue these discourses and come to my Childhood againe I remember this defluction at my Eares abovementioned continued in that
Uiolence That my Freinds did not think fitt to teach mee soe much
as my Alphabett, till I was seauen yeare old at what tyme my

defluction Ceased and left me free of the disease my Anncestors were subiect vnto being the *Epalepsie*; My schoolemaster in the house of my said Lady Grandmother began then to teach mee the Alphabet and afterwards Grammar and other bookes commonly reade in schooles In which I profited soe much That at the end of two yeares I attained the knowledge of the Lattaine Tongue In soe much that vpon this Theme, *Audaces fortuna juvat*, I made an oration of a sheete of paper and fifty or three score verses in the space of one day! I remember in that tyme I was corrected sometymes for going to Cuffs with two schoolefellows or some other shrewd boys Trick, being both elder then my selfe; but neuer for telling Lye or any other Fault, My naturall disposition and inclination being soe Contrary to all falshood That being demaunded whether I had committed any fault whereof I might bee justly suspected, I did vse euer to confesse it freely, and therevpon choosed rather to suffer Correction then to staine my minde with telling a Lye which I did iudge then noe tyme could euer deface And I can affirme to all the World truly, That from my first Infancy to this houre I tould not willingly any thing that was false, my soule naturally having an Antipathy to lying and deceipt. After I had attained the Age of nine (during all which time I lived in my said Lady Grandmothers house at Eyton) my Parents thought fitt to send mee to some place where I might learne the Welch Tongue as beleeving it necessary to enable mee to treate with those of my freinds and Tennants who vnderstood noe other Language, wherevpon I was recommended to Mr. Edward Thellwall of Placeward in Denbighshire. This Gentleman I must remember with honor as having of himselfe acquired the exact knowledge of Greeke Lattaine Frensh Italian and Spanish and all other Learning, Having for that purpose neither gone beyond seas nor soe much as had the benefitt of any Vniversityes. Besides he was of that rare Temper in governing his Choller That I neuer sawe him angry during the tyme of my stay there, and haue heard soe much of him for many yeares before when occasion of offence was giuen him. I haue seene him redden in the Face, and after remaine for a while Silent, But when he spake, his words were soe calme and gentle,

That I found he had digisted his Coller, Though yet I confesse I could neuer attaine that Perfection as being subiect euer to Choller and Passion more then I ought and generally to speake my mynde freely and indeed rather to imitate those who having fire within doores chuse rather to giue it vent then suffer it to burne the house. I commend yet much more the Manner of Mr. Thellwall, and certainly he that can forbeare speaking for some while will remitt much of his Passion, But as I could not learne much of him in this kynde soe I did as litle profitt in Learning the Welch or any other of those Languages that worthy Gentleman vnderstood as having a Tertian Ague for the most part of nine moneths which was all the time I staid in his house. Having recovered my strength againe I was sent, (being about the Age of ten) to bee taught by one Mr. Newton at Diddlebury in Shropshire where in the space of lesse then two yeares I not onely recovered all I had lost in my sicknes But attained to the Knowledge of the Greeke Tongue and Logick In soe much That at twelue yeare old my Parents thought fitt to send mee to Oxford to Vniuersity Colledge,[1] where I remember to haue disputed at my first coming in Logick and to haue made in Greeke the Exercises required in that Colledge oftner then in Lattaine. I had not beene many moneths in the Vniuersity but news was brought mee of my Fathers death, his Sicknes being a Lethargie Caros or Coma uigilans[2] which continued long vpon him; he seemed at last to dye without much paine though in his Senses. Vpon opinion giuen by Phisitians That his disease was mortall my Mother thought fitt to send for mee home, And presently after my Fathers death to desire her Brother Sir Francis Newport to hasten to London to obtayne my wardshippe for his and her vse joyntly; which hee obtayned; Shortly after I was sent againe to my Studyes in Oxford where I had not beene long, but that an Overture for a Match with the daughter and heire of Sir William Herbert of St. Gillians[3] was made The occasion whereof was this; Sir William Herbert being heire male to the Old Earle of Penbrook aboue mentioned by a younger sonne of his (for the elder sonne had a daughter who carried away those greate Posessions the Earle of Worcester now houlds in Monmouthshire) as I said before having one onely daughter superviving made a will whereby hee estated all his Posessions in Monmouthshire and Ireland vpon his said daughter, upon Condition she maried one of the sur-name of Herbert, Otherwise the said Lands to descend to the heires Male of the said Sir William and his Daughter to haue onely a small portion out of the Lands he had in Anglesey and Carnarvanshire, His lands being thus setled Sir William dyed shortly afterwards: He was a man much Conversant with bookes and especially given to the Study of Divinity In soe much, That he writt an Exposition vpon the Revelation which is printed, Though some thought he was as farre from finding the Sense thereof as he was from Attaining the Philosophers stone which was another part of his Study. Howsoeuer he was very vnderstanding in all other things; he was noted yet to bee of a very high minde, But I can say litle of him as having neuer seene his person, nor otherwise had much information concerning him. His daughter and Heire called Mary after her father dyed continued vnmarried till shee was one and twenty none of the Herberts appearing in all that tyme who either in Age or fortune was fitt to Match her;[1] About this tyme I had attained the Age of fifteene And a Match at last being proposed yet notwithstanding the Dis-parity of yeares betwixt vs vpon the 28th of February 1598 in the house of Eyton where the same man (Viccar of Vroxeter)[2] that married my Father and mother Christned and married me. Not long after my mariag I went againe to Oxford together with my wife and Mother who tooke a house and lived for a certayne tyme there. And now having a due remedy for that Lasciviousnes to which youth is naturally inclined I followed my booke more Close then euer In which course I continued till I attained about the Age of Eighteene, when my Mother tooke a house in London betweene which place and Mountgomery Castle I passed my Time till I came to the Age of one and twenty having in that space divers children whereof none yet live to this day, I having now none remayning but Beatrice, Richard and Edward; During this tyme of living in the Vniuersity or at home, I did without any Master or Teacher Attaine the Knowledge of the Frensh Italian and Spanish, Languages by the helpe of some bookes in Lattaine or English translated into those Idiums and the Dictionaryes of those seuerall Languages. I attaind also to sing my part at first sight in Musicke, and to play on the Lute with very litle or almost noe teaching. My Intention in Learning Languages being to make my selfe a Citizen of the world as farr as it were possible, and my learning of Musicke was for this end that I might entertaine my selfe at home and together refresh my mynde after my studyes to which I was exceedingly inclined, and that I might not neede the company of younge men in whome I obserued in those tymes much ill example and deboist.[1]

Being gotten thus farre into my Age, I shall giue some obseruations concerning ordinary Education; euen from the first Infancy vntill the departure from the Vniuersity As being desirous (together with the Narration of my life) to deliuer such rules as I conceiue may bee usefull to my posterity; And first I finde That in the Infancy Those diseases are to bee remedied which may bee hereditary vnto them on either side, Soe that if they bee subiect to the Stone or Grauell I doe conceiue it will bee good for the Nurse sometimes to drinke Posset drinkes in which are boyld such things as are good to expell Grauell and Stone; The Childe also him selfe when hee comes to some age may vse the same Posset drinks; Of herbes good for the Stone are many Reckoned by the Phisitians of which also my selfe could bring a large Catologue but rather leaue it to those who are expert in that Arte; The same Course is to bee taken for the Goult, for which purpose I doe much comend the Bathing of Childrens leggs and feete in the water wherein the Smiths quench theire Iron as also water wherein Allam hath been infused or boyled as also the decocktion of Juniper Berryes and Bayberries Ckamoedris Chamoepetis,[2] Which Bathes also are good for those that are hereditaryly subiect to the Paldsje for these things doe much strengthen the Sinews, as also Olium Castorij, and Succoni,[3] which are not to be used without Advice: They that are also subiect to the Spleene from theire Anncestors ought to vse these herbes that are Splenetiques, and those that are troubled with the falling Sicknes with Cephaniques, Of which certainly I should haue had neede but for the Purging of my Eares abouementioned. Breefely, what disease soeuer it bee That is deriued from Anncestors of either side, It will bee necessary first to giue such medicines to the Nurse as may make her milk effectuall for those purposes, As also afterwards to give vnto the Childe it selfe such specifique remedyes as his age and Constitution will beare; I could say much more vpon this Poynt, as hauing delighted euer in the Knowledge of herbes Plants and Gumbs and in few words the History of Nature. In soe much That coming to Apothecaryes Shopps It was my ordinary manner when I looked vpon the Bills filed vp contayning the Phisitians Prescriptions to tell euery mans disease, Howbeit I shall not presume in these particulars to prescribe to my Posterity, thoughe I beleiue I know the best receipts for almost all diseases, but shall leaue them to the Expert Physitian, Onely I will recommend againe to my Posterity the Curing of hereditary diseases in the very Infancy, otherwise without much difficulty they will neuer bee Cured.

When Children goe to schoole they should haue one to attend them who may take Care of theire manners as well as the Schoolemaster doth of theire Learning, for among boyes all Uice is easily learned, And here I could wish it constantly obserued, That neither the Master should Correct him for faults of his manners nor his Gouernor for manners for the faults in his Learning. After the Alphabet is taught I like well the shortest and cleerest Grammars and such bookes Into which all the Greeke and Lattaine words are seuerally Contriued, In which kynde one Comenus[1] hath given an Example; This being done It would bee much better to proceede with Greeke Authors nor with Lattaine, for as it is as easy to learne at first the one as the other It would bee much better to giue the first impressions into the Childes memory of those things which are more rare and vnvsuall: Therefore I would haue them begin at Greeke first And the rather that there is not that Art in the world wherein the Greekes haue not excelled and gone before others Soe that when you looke vpon Philosophy Astronomy Mathematicks Medicine and breifly all learning the Greekes haue exceeded all Nations; When he shalbe ready to goe to the Vniuersity It will bee fitt also his

Gouernor for manners goe along with him. It being the fraile nature of youths as they growe to ripenes in Age to bee more Capable of doing ill, vnlesse theire manners bee well guided and themselues by degrees habituated in Uertue, with which if once they acquaint themselves they will finde more pleasure in it then euer they can doe in Uice Since euery body loves vertuous persons whereas the Uitious doe scarce love one another. For this purpose it will bee necessary That yee keepe the Company of graue learned men who are of good Reputation and heare rather what they say and imitate what they doe then follow the example of young wilde and rash persons; And certainly of those two parts which are to bee acquired in youth whereof one is goodnes and vertuous manners, the other learning and knowledge I shall soe much preferre the first before the second as I shall euer thinke vertue accompanied with ordinary discretion will make his way better both to happines in this world and the next then any puft knowledge which would cause him to bee either Insolent and vayne glorious or minister (as it were) Armes and Advantages to him for doing a Mischeife, soe that it is pitty that wicked dispositions should haue knowledge to accuate[1] theire Ill Intentions or Courage to maintaine them, That Fortitude which should defend all a Mans vertues being neuer well imployed to defend his humors Passions or Uices. I doe not approue for Elder Brothers That Course of study which is ordinary vsed in the Vniuersity, which is if theire Parents perchaunce intend they shall stay there fowre or five yeares to imploy the said Time as if they meant to proceede Masters of Art and Doctors in some Science, for which purpose theire Tutors comonly spend much tyme in teaching them the subtilityes of Logicke which as it is vsually practized enables them for litle more then to bee excellent wranglers, which Art though it may bee tollerable in a mercenary Lawyer I can by noe meanes commend it in a sober and well gouerned Gentleman. I approue much those parts of Logicke which teach men to deduce theire proofes from firme and vndoubted principles and show men to distinguish betwixt truth and Falshood and help them to discouer Fallasies, sophismes, and that which the Schoolemen call vitious Argumentations,

Concerning which I shall not enter here into a Long discourse; Soe much of Logick as may serue for this purpose being acquired, some good Summe of Philosophye may bee learned, which may teach him the Ground both of the Platonick and Arestotelian Philosophy. After which It will not bee amisse to reade The *Idea Medecinae Philosophicae* written by Severnius Danus[1] there being many things considerable concerning the Paracelsian principles written in that booke which are not found in former writers. It will not bee amisse also to reade over *Franciscus Patricius* and *Tilesius*, who haue examined and contraverted[2] the ordinary perepateticke Doctrine, All which may bee performed in one yeare, That terme being enough for Philosophy as I conceiue and six moneths for Logick for I am Confident a man may haue quickly more then hee needes of those two arts. These being attained It will bee fitt to study Geography with exactnes soe much as may teach a Man the scituation of all Countreys in the wholle world together with which It will bee requisite to learne something concerning the Gouerments manners and Religions either Anncient or new as also the Interests of state and Relations in Amity or strength in which they stand to theire Neighbours. It will bee necessary also at the same time to learne the vse of the Celestiall globe, The studyes of both Globes being complicated and ioyned together. I doe not conceiue yet the knowledge of judiciall Astrologie soe necessary but onely for generall predictions, particular Events being neither intended by nor collected out of the Starres. It will be fitt also to learne Arithmatick and Geometry in some good measure but especially Arithmaticke as being most vsefull for many purposes and among the rest for keeping of Accompt, where there is much vse; As for the knowledge of Lynes superficies and bodyes though it bee a science of much Certainty and demonstration it is not much vsefull for a Gentleman vnlesse it bee to vnderstand Fortification, The knowledge whereof is worthy of those who intend the warres, Though yet he must remember That whatsoeuer Art doth in way of Defence Art likewise in the way of Assayling can destroy. This study hath Cost mee much Labour but as yet I could never find how any place could be so fortified but that there were means in

The Gunpowder Plot conspirators and their execution in 1606; German engraving c. 1606

certain opposite Lines to prevent or subvert all that could be done in that kind. It will become a gentleman to have some knowledge in Medicine, especially the Diagnostick part, whereby he may take timely notice of a disease, and by that means timely prevent it, as also the prognostick part whereby he may judge of the Symphomes either increasing or decreasing in the disease, as also concerning the Crisis or Indication thereof. This art will get a Gentleman not only much knowledge but much credit, since seeing any sick body he will be able to tell in all human probibility whether he shall recover, or if he shall die of the disease, to tell what signes shall go before and what the conclusion will be; it will become him also to know not only the ingredients but Doses of certain Cathartique or purging, Emetique, or Vomotive medicines, specifique or cholerique, melancholique, or phlegmatique constitutions, phlebotomy being only necessary for those who abound in blood, besides I would have a Gentleman know how to make these medicines himself, and afterwards prepare them with his own hands, it being the manner of Apothecaries so frequently to put in the Succidania[1] that no man is sure to find with them medicines made with the true drugs which ought to enter into the Composition when it is Exotique or rarc, or when they are extant in the shop no man can be assured that the said drugs are not rotten, or that they have not lost their natural force and vertue. I have studied this art very much also, and have in case of extremity ministred physick with that success which is strange, whereof I shall give two or three examples: Richard Griffiths of Sutton my servant being sick of a malignant pestilent feaver,[2] and tryed in vain all our Country Physitians could do, and his water at last stinking so griveously, which Physitians note to be a signe of extention of natural heat, and consequently of present death, I was intreated to see him, when as yet he had neither eaten, drank, slept, or known any body for the space of six or seven days, whereupon demanding whether the Physitians had given him over, and it being answered unto me that they had, I said it would not be amiss to give him the quantity of an haslenut of a certain rare receipt which I had, assuring that if any thing in the world could recover him, that would: of which I said I was so confident that I would come the next day at four of the clock in the afternoon unto him, and at that time I doubted not but they should find signes of amendment. I provided they should put the doses I gave them being about the bigness of a nut down his throat, which being done with much difficulty, I came the morrow after at the hour appointed, when to the wonder of his family he knew me and asked for some broth, and not long after recover'd. My cozen Athelston Owen also of Rhue Sayson,[1] having an Hydrocephale also in that extremity that his eyes began to start out of his head and his tongue to come out of his mouth, and his whole head finally exceeding its natural proportion, in so much that his Physitians likewise left him; I prescribed to him the decoction of two Diuretique Rootes, which after he had drank four or five days, he urin'd in that abundance that his head by degrees returned to its ancient figure, and all other signes of health appeared, whereupon also he wrote a Letter to me that he was so suddainly and perfectly restored to his former health, that it seemed more like a miracle than a cure; for those are the very words in the Letter he sent me. I cured a great Lady in London of an Issue of blood when all the Physitians had given her over with so easy a medicine that the Lady herself was astonished to find the effects thereof. I could give more examples in this kind, but these shall suffice; I will for the rest deliver a Rule I conceive for finding out the best receipts not only for curing all inward but outward hurts, such as are Ulcers, Tumors, contusions, wounds, and the like: you must look upon all Pharmacopaeia's or Antidataries[2] or several Countries; of which sort I have in my Library the Pharmacopaeia Londinensis, Parisensis, Amstelodamensis, that of Quercsetau, Bauderaui, Renedeus, Valerius Scordus, Pharmacopaeia Coloniensis, Augustana, Venetiana, Vononiensis, Florentina, Romana, Messanensis.[3] In some of which are told not only what the Receipts there set down are good for, but the Doses of them. The Rule I here give is, that what all the said Dispensatories, Antidataries, or Pharmacopaeias prescribe as effectuall for overcoming a disease is certainly good, for as they are set forth by the authority of the Physitians of these several Countries, what they all ordain must necessarily be effectual, but they who will follow my advice shall find in that litle short Antidotary called Amstelodamensis not long since put forth almost all that is necessary to be known for curing of diseases, wounds &c. There is a book called Aurora Medicorum[1] very fit to be read in this kind. Among writers of Physick, I do especially commend after Hipocrates and Gallen, Fernelius,[2] Lud: Mercatus, and Dan: Sennertus, and Heurnius;[3] I could name many more, but I conceive these may suffize. As for the Chymique or Spagerique[4] medicines I cannot commend them to the vse of my Posterity, there being neither Emetique, Cathortique, Diaphoretique, or Diuretique, medicines extant among them which are not much more happily and safely performed by vegitable, but hereof enough since I pretend noe further then to give some few directions to my posterity. In the meane while I conceive it is a fine Study and worthy a Gentleman to bee a good Botanique that soe hee may know the nature of all herbes and plants being our fellow Creatures and made for the vse of man, for which purpose it will bee fitt for him to cutt out of some good herball all the Icones[5] together with the descriptions of them of the Herbes there and to lay by themselues all such as growe in England And afterwards to select againe such as vsually Growe by the high way side, in Meadows, by Rivers or in Marshes or in Cornefields or in dry and Mountanous places or in Rocks, walls, or in shady places such as growe by the seaside, for this being done and the said Icones ordinarily carried by themselues or by theire servants one may presently finde out euery herbe he meetes withall, especially if the said Flowers be truly coloured. Afterwards It will not bee amisse to distinguish by themselues such herbes as are in Gardens and are Exotiques and transplanted hither: As for those plants which will not endure our Clyme though the knowledge of them bee worthy of a Gentleman and the vertues of them fitt to bee learned especially if they bee brought over to a Droggest as medicinall yet the Icones of them are not soe pertinent to bee knowne as the former vnlesse it bee where there is daunger of adulterating the said Medicaments In which Case it is good to haue Recourse, not only to the Botaniques but also to Gesnars[6] dispensatory and to *Aurora medicorum* abovementioned being bookes which teach a man to distinguish between good and bad drogues; And thus much of Medicine may not onely be vsefull but dilectable to a Gentleman since which way soeuer he passeth he may finde something to entertayne him. I must noe lesse commend the study of Anotamy which whosoeuer Considers I belieue will neuer be an Atheist, The Frame of mans body and Coherence of his parts being soe strange and paradoxall That I hould it to bee the greatest miracle of Nature; though when all is done I doe not finde shee hath made it so much as proofe against one pin lest it should bee thought she made it noe less then prison to the Soul.

Having thus past ouer all humane Literature It will bee fitt to say something of morall vertues and Theologicall learning. As for the first since the Christians and the Heathens are in a manner agreed concerning the definitions of Uertues It would not bee inconvenient to begin with those definitions which Aristotle in his Moralls hath giuen as being confirmed for the most part by the Platonique, Stoiques, and other Philosophers, and in generall by the Christian Church as well as all Nations in the World whatsoeuer, They being Doctrines imprinted in the soule in its first originall and Contayning the Principall and first notices by which man may attaine his happines here or hereafter, there being noe man that is giuen to Uice That doth not finde much Opposition both in his owne Conscience and in the Religion and Lawe as taught elsewhere, And This I dare say That a vertuous man may not onely goe securely through all the Religions but all the Lawes in the world and whatsoeuer obstructions he meete obtayne both an Jnward peace and outward wellcome among all with whome hee shall negotiate or Converse.[1] This vertue therefore I shall recommend to my Posterity as the greatest perfection he can attaine vnto in this life and the plege of eternall happines hereafter, there being none that can iustly hope of an vnion with the supreme God That doth not come as neare to him in this life by vertue and goodnes as he can, Soe that if humane Frailty doe Interrupt this Vnion by comitting faults that make him vncapable of his euerlasting happines It will bee fitt by a serious Repentance to expiate and emaculate[1] those faults and for the rest trust to the mercy of God his Creator Redeemer and preseruer, who being our Father (and knowing well in what weake Condition through Infirmities wee are), will I doubt not Commiserate those Transgressions wee commit when they are done without desire to Offend his Devine Maiesty and together Rectify our vnderstanding through his Grace, since wee comonly sinne through noe other Cause but that wee mistooke a true good for that which was onely apparent and soe were deceiued by making an vndue Election in the obiects proposed to vs wherein though it will bee fitt for euery man to Confesse That hee hath offended an Infinite Maiesty and Power, yet as vpon better Consideration he findes he did not meane infinitely to offend there will bee iust reason to belieue That God will not inflict an infinite punishment vpon him if hee bee truly penitent soe that his Justice may bee satisfied if not with mans Repentance yet at least with some temporall Punishment here or hereafter such as may bee Proportionable to the Offence; though I cannot deny but when man would jnfinitely offend God in a despite-full and contemptuous way It will bee but iust that he suffer an Jnfinite Punishment But as I hope none are soe wicked as to sinne purposedly and with a high hand against the eternall Maiesty of God Soe when they shall commit any sinnes out of Frailty I shall beleiue either that vnlesse they bee finally impenitent and as they say ingeniously sould over to Sinne, Gods mercy will accept of theire Endeavors to returne into a right way and soe make theire peace with him by all those good meanes that are possible. Having thus recommended the Learning of morall Philosophy and Practice of Uertue as the most necessary knowledge and vsefull exercise of mans life I shall obserue That euen in the imploying of our Uertues, Discretion is required, for euery vertue is not promiscuously to bee vsed but such onely as is proper for the present occasion. Therefore though a warye and discreete wisdome bee most vsefull where noe imminent danger appeares, yet where an Enemy draweth his sword against you, you shall haue most vse of Fortitude, Prevention being too late when the danger is pressing. On the other side There is noe Occasion to vse your Fortitude against

wrongs done by women, children or ignorant persons, That I may
say nothing of those who are magistrates and much your superiors
since you might by a discreete wisdome haue declyned the Iniury
or when it were too late to doe soe you may with a more equall
minde support That which is done either by Authority in the One
or frailty in the other. And certainly to such kynde of Persons
Forgivenes will bee proper; In which kinde I am confident noe man
of my Time hath exceeded mee for though whensoeuer my Honor
hath beene engaged noe man hath euer beene more forward o
hazard his life, yet where with my honor J could Forgive I neuer
vsed Revenge as leaving it always to God, who the lesse I punish
mine Enemyes will inflict soe much the more Punishment on them,[1]
And to this Forgiuenes of others Three Considerations have specially
invited mee.

   1. That hee that cannot forgiue others breake the Bridge ouer
which he must passe himselfe for euery man had neede to bee forgiuen.

   2. That when a man wants or comes short of an intire and accom-
plished vertue our defects may bee supplyed this way Since forgiving
of evill deedes in others amounteth to noe lesse then vertue in vs:
That therefore that it may bee not vnaptly called the paying our
Debts with another mans money;

   3. That it is the most necessary and proper worke of euery man,
for though when I doe not a iust thing or a Charitable or a wise
another man may doe it for mee yet noe man can forgiue my Enemy
but my selfe and these haue beene the Cheife motives for which I
haue beene euer inclined to forgivenes whereof though I haue rarely
found other effects Then that my servants Tennants and Neighbours
haue therevpon more frequently offended mee, yet at least I haue
had within mee an inward Peace and comfort thereby Since I can
truly say nothing euer gaue my mynde more ease then when I had
forgiuen my Enemyes and being that which freed mee from many
Cares and Perturbations which otherwise would haue molested mee.

   And this likewise brings in another Rule concerning the vse of
Uertues which is That you are not to vse Iustice where Mercy is

most proper as on the other side a foolish pitty is not to bee preferred before that which is iust and necessary for good Example. Soe likewise Liberality is not to bee vsed where Parcimony or Frugality is more requisite, as on the other side It willbee but a sordide thing in a Gentleman to spare where the expending of money would acquire vnto him Advantage credit or honor, And this Rule in generall ought to bee practized that the vertue requisite vnto the Occasion is euer to bee produced as the most opportune and necessary. That therefore wisdome is the Soule of all vertues giving them as vnto her members life and Motion and soe necessary in euery action That whosoeuer by the benefit of true wisdome makes vse of the Right vertue on all emergent occasions I dare say would neuer bee constrained to haue recourse to Uice, whereby it appeares That every vertue is not to bee imployed indifferently but that onely which is proper for the busines in Question, among which yet Temperance seemes so vniuersally requisite That some part of it at least willbee a necessary Ingredient in all humane Actions, Since there may bee an Excesse euen in Religious worship at those tymes when other dutyes are required at our hands. After all, moral vertues are learned and directed to the service and glory of God as the principall end and vse of them.

It would bee fitt that some time bee spent in learning of Rhetorique or Oratory to the intent that vpon all Occasions you may express yourselfe with Eloquence and Grace, For as it is not enough for a man to haue a Diamond vnlesse it bee pollisht and cutt out into its due angles above and a foyle bee sett vnderneath whereby it may the better transmitt and vibrate its native lustre and Rayes, Soe it will not bee sufficient for a man to haue a greate vnderstanding in all matters vnlesse the said vnderstanding bee not onely polished and cleare in the definitions and divisions belonging to any art but well vnderset and illustrated with those Figueres Tropes and collours which Rhetorique affords where there is vse of Perswasion. I can by noe meanes yet commend an affected eloquence there being nothing soe pedanticall or indeed that would giue more Suspition that the Truth is not intended then to vse overmuch the Comon formes prescribed in schools. It is well said by them yet That there are two parts of Eloquence Necessary and Recommendable; One is to speake hard things plainly soe that when a knotty or intricate busines hauing noe method or Coherence in its parts shall bee presented It will bee a singular part of Oratory to take those parts in sunder set them together aptly and soe exhibite them to the vnderstanding. And this part of Rhetorique I much commend to euery body, there being noe true vse of speech but to make things cleare perspicuous and manifest which otherwise would bee perplext doubtfull and obscure.

The other part of Oratory is to speake common things ingeniously or wittily there being noe litle vigor and Force added to words when they are deliuered in a Neate and fine way and somewhat out of the Ordinary Rode, common and dull language Relishing more of the Clowne then of the Gentleman but herein also Affectation must bee avoyded, it being better for a man by a Native and cleare Eloquence to expresse himselfe then by those words which may smell either of the Lampe or Inkhorne soe that in generall one may obserue That men who Fortify and vphold theire speeches with strong and euident Reasons haue euer operated more in the minds of Auditors then those who haue made Rhetoricall Excursions.

And certainly it will bee better for a man who is doubtfull of his pay to take an ordinary siluer piece with its due stamp vpon it, then an Extraordinarye guilded piece which may perchance contayne a baser mettle vnder it, and to prefer a well favoured whollsome woman though with a Tawny Complexion before a besmeared and painted face.

It is a generall Note That a mans witt is best shewed in his answer and his valour in his defence, that therefore as men learne in Fencing how to ward all blowes and thrusts which are or can bee made against him, Soe it will bee fitting to debate and resolue before hand what you are to say or doe vpon any Affront giuen you, least otherwise you should bee Surprized; Arestotle hath written of Rhetoriques a worke in my opinion not inferior to his best pieces whome therefore with Cicero de Oratore and Quintilian[1] you may reade for your Instruction how to speake. Neither of which two yet I can thinke soe exact in theire Orations but That a middle stile will bee of more efficacy, Cicero in my opinion being too long and tedious and Quintilian too short and Concise.

Having thus by morall Philosophy enabled your selfe to all that wisdome and Goodnes which is requisite to direct you in your particular Actions, It will bee fitt now to think how you are to behaue yourselfe as a publique person or member of the Comon wealth and Kingdome wherein you live, as also to looke into those principles and Grounds vpon which government is framed, it being manifest in Nature that the wise doth easily governe the foolish, and the strong Master the weake, Soe that he that could Attaine most wisdome and power would quickly rule his fellow, for proofe whereof One may obserue That when a King is sicke during that Time The Phisitian Gouerns him, and in the day of Battle an expert generally appoints the King a Place in which he shall stand which was annciently the office of the Conestables de Fraunce; In Lawe also the Iudge is in a sort superior to his King as long as hee judgeth be-twixt him and his people. In divinity also he to whome the King comitts the Charge of his Conscience is his superior in that par-ticular. All which instances may sufficiently prove that in many Cases the wiser gouernes or commands one lesse wise then himselfe, vnlesse a willfull obstinacy bee Interposed, In which case recourse must bee had to strength where Obedience is necessary.

Concerning Religion I thought it my best Course to begin vpon the most certaine and vnfallible Principles I could finde and from thence to proceede vnto the next. Having therefore considered whether in all the Religions I could meete with anncient or moderne there were any Poynts or Articles soe vniuersally taught That they were not questioned or doubted of in any other Religion I obserued these five onely to bee Catholique and vniuersall 1: That there is one supreme God. 2. That he is to be worshipped. 3. That vertue and Piety ioyned with Faith in and love of God are the best ways to serue and worship him. 4. That wee ought to Repent vs of our Sinnes and seriously to returne to God and the Right way. 5. That there is reward and Punishment both in this life and after it. Having established these Foundations in my selfe I inquired concerning the Poynts or Articles added vnto them And as here I found many things vrged which did Depend meerely vpon the Credit and Authority of certaine Churches which did not sufficiently agree and Cohere among themselues. I found that either I must studye Contrauersies in all Languages Countreys and Times which were an Jnfinite and impossible Labour, Or otherwise That I must insist cheifly vpon these five Catholique poynts as the most knowne and generally confessed meanes of coming to God. I did not doubt yet but God in his Mercy might and did in seuerall Ages and Countreys (by diuers extraordinary wayes) manifest his wisdome power and goodness; To the Relations whereof therefore I thought fitt to giue a Reuerence and pious beleife, Howbeit as most of these Doctrines were with much Uehemency and Bitterness on all sides disputed I thought as before That it was an endles worke for mee or any other Laike to examine them according to all theire parts, when yet it were our duty to inquire into such matters as were soe farre beyond our Reach and Capacity. Houlding my selfe therefore principally to these five Catholique Articles, I did nonethelesse to my vttermost embrace and beleive all that the Church in which I was borne and brought vp did vniformely teach, sequestring and dismissing onely the Contrauerted points to those who had either will leasure or meanes to study them sufficiently, Resolving yet That if any poynts of Faith wheresoeuer taught were once inserted or inoculated into my five Catholique Poynts as necessary parts or branches thereof to receive them with One credit and Assent but those especially which implyed noe contradiction. To conclude I insisted cheifely vpon my five Catholique Articles for these reasons. 1. That there was noe other open and manifest way declared to all mankinde whereby to establish Gods vniversall Providence which is his highest Attribute; 2. That I found nothing could bee added to them which could make a man Really more vertuous and good when the afforesaid five points were rightly explicated; 3. That though the Doctrins added therevnto were indeed comfortable and full of promis to those who beleived them, yet that they were more Contrauerted then that the Age of any man could vnty and disolve the Knotts and Jntricaces in them, or indeede soe much as reade the seuerall Authors which had written concerning that Argument without which yet hee could not say hee had heard all partyes or was able to forme a sufficient Judgment vpon them; 4. That I found all Misteryes Sacraments and Revelations cheefely tended to the Establishment of these five Articles as being at least the principall end for which they were ordeyned; 5. That I thought That the doing some good deede, speaking some good word or thinking some good thought were more necessary exercises of my life then that I should Intermitt them for any Consideration whatsoeuer; Vpon these five poynts therefore I insisted beleiving the rest either piously vpon the Authority of the Church or at least doubting piously when proofes were not sufficiently made and confirmed vnto mee. But herein as a Laike I intend onely to giue the reasons of my beleifc without prescribing rules to any other.

The Exerciscs I cheifely vsed and most recomend to my Posterity, were riding the greate horse[1] and Fencing, In which Arts I had excellent Masters English Frensh and Italian. As for Dancing I could neuer finde leasure enough to learne it as imploying my minde alwayes in Acquiring of some Art or Science more vsefull, Howbeit I shall wish these three Exercises learned in this Order:

That dancing may bee learned first as that which doth Fashion the body giues one a good presence in and addresse to all Companyes since it disposeth the Lims to a Kind of Souplesse (as the Frenshmen call it) and Agillity, in soe much as they seem to haue the Vse of theire Leggs armes and bodyes more then any others that standing stiff and starke in theire Postures seeme as if they were taken in theire Joynts or had not the perfect vse of theire members: I speake not this yet as if I would haue a youth neuer stand still in Company, but onely that when he hath occasion to stirre his motions may bee comely and gracefull, That he may learne to know how to come in and goe out of a Roome where company is, how to make Courtesies handsomly, according to the seuerall degrees of persons he shall encounter, how to putt of and hold his hatt, All which and many other things which become men are taught by the more accurate Dancing Masters in France.

The next Exercise a young man should learne (but not before he is eleuen or twelue yeares of Age) should be Fencing, For the Attayning of which The Frenshmans rule is excellent Bon pied Bonœil by which to teach men how farre they may stretch out theire Feete when they would make a thrust against theire Enemy least either they should overstride themselves, or not striding farr enough faile to bring the poynt of theire weapon home. The second Part of his direction aduiseth the Scholler to keep a Fixt eye vpon the Poynt of his Enemyes sword, to the intent he may both put by or ward the blowes and Thrusts made against him and together direct the Poynt of his Sword vpon some part of his Enemy that lyeth naked and open to him: The good fencing Masters in France especially when they present a Foyle or Fleuret[1] to their Schollers tell him It hath two parts, One which he calleth the Fort or strong and the other the Foyble or weake; with the Fort or strong which extendes from the part of the hillt next the Sword about a third part of the wholle leangth thereof, he teacheth his Schollers to defend themselues and put by and ward the Thrusts and blowes of his Enemy. And with the other two third parts to strike or thrust as he shall see occasion: which rule also teacheth how to strike or thrust high or Lowe as his Adversary doth and breifely to take his measure and tyme vpon his Adversaryes motions whereby he may both defend himselfe and offend his Aduersary, Of which I have had much experiment and vse both in the Fleuret or Foyle as also when I fought in good earnest with many persons at one and the same time as will appeare in the Sequell of my life. And indeed I think I shall not speake vaine gloriously of my selfe If I say that noe man vnderstood the vse of his weapon better then I did or hath more dexterously prevailed himselfe thereof on all occasions since I found noe man could be hurt but through some Error in Fencing.

I spent much tyme also in learning to ride the greate horse, that creature being made aboue all others for the service of man, as affording his rider all the Advantages of which he is Capable, while Some-times hee giues him Strength, sometimes Agillity or Motion for the Overcoming of his Enemy In soe much That a good Rider on a good Horse is as much aboue himselfe and others as this world can make him. The Rule for gracefull ryding is That a Man hould his Eyes always betwixt the two Eares and his rod over the left eare of his horse which he is to vse for turning him euery way, helping him selfe with his left foote and rod vpon the left part of his necke, to make his horse turne on the right hand, and with the right foote and help of his rod[1] also (if neede be) to turn him on the left hand, But this to bee vsed rather when one would make a Horse vnderstand these motions then when he is a ready horse the foote and stirrop alone, applyed to either shoulder being sufficient with the help of the Raynes to make him turne any way; That a Ryder thus may haue the vse of his sword, or when it is requisite onely to make a horse goe sideward It will bee enough to keepe the Raines equall in his hand and with the flatt of his Legge and foote together and touch vpon the shoulder of the horse with his stirropp to make him goe sideward either way, without either Aduancing forward or retyring backwards.

The most vsefull Aer as the Frenchmen terme it is Terreterra; the Courbettes, Cabrioles, un pas et un sault[2] being fitter for horses of Parade and Triumph then for Souldiers yet I cannot deny but a Demivolte[3] with Courbettes soe that they bee not too high may be vsefull in a fight or Meslee for as Labroue hath it in his booke of Horsemanship[4] Monsieur de Montmorency having a horse That was excellent in performing the Demyvolte did with his sword strike downe two Aduersaryes from theire horses in a Tournay where diuers of the Prime Gallants from France did meete; For taking his tyme when the horse was in the haight of his Courtbetta and dis-charging a blowe then his sword fell with such weight and force vpon two Cavelliers one after another that he stroke them from theire horses to the Ground.

The manner of fighting a Duell on horseback I was taught thus: wee had each of vs a reasonable stiffe riding rod in our hands about the length of a sword and soe rid one against the other, hee as the more expert saught still to passe mee and then to get behinde mee and after to Turne with his right hand vpon my left side with his rod that soe hee might hitt mee with the poynt thereof in the body. And he that can doe this handsomly is sure to overcome his Aduersary, It being Impossible to bring his sword about enough to defend himselfe or offend the Assaylant, and to get this Advantage which they call in Frensh Gaigner la crouppe, nothing is soe vsefull as to make a horse go only sideward till his Aduersary bee past him Since he will by this meanes both avoyd his Aduersarys blow or thrust and on a suddaine get on the left hand of his Aduersary in the manner I formerly related. But of this Art let Labroue and Pluuinel[1] bee read who are excellent Masters in that Arte of whome I must confesse I learned much though to speake ingeniously my breaking two or three Coults and teaching them afterwards those Aers of which they were most capable taught mee both what I was to doe and made mee see my Errors more then all theire precepts.

To make a horse fitt for the Warrs and embolden him against all Terrors these Inventions are vsefull, To beate a Drumme out of the stable first and then give him his Provender, Then beate a Drumme in the stable by degrees and then giue him his Provender vpon the Drumme. When hee is acquainted herewith sufficiently you must shoote of a Pistoll out of the stable before he hath his Provender; then you may shoote of a Pistoll in the stable and soe by degrees bring it as neare to him as you can till hee bee acquainted with the Pistoll, likewise remembring still after euery shott to giue him more Prouender. You must also cause his Groome to put on bright Armor and soe to rubb his heeles and dresse him. You must also present a sword before him in the said Armor and when you haue done giue him still more provender, Lastly his Ryder must bring this horse forth into the open feild where a bright Armor must bee fastned vpon a stake and set forth in the likenes of an Armed man as much as is possible which being done the rider must put his horse on till hee make him not onely approach the said image but throw it downe, after which you must bee sure to giue him some prouender

34

that hee may bee encouraged to doe the like against an Aduersary in Battaile. It will bee good also that two men doe hould vp a Cloake betwixt them in the feild and then the rider to put the horse to it till hee leape ouer, which Cloake also they may raise as they see occasion when the horse is able to leape soe high. You shall doe well also to vse your horse to swimming which you may doe either by trayling him after you at the Tayle of a Boate in a good river, holding him by the head at the length of the bridle or by putting a good swimmer in a Lynnen Wastecoate and breeches vpon him.

It will bee fitt for a Gentleman also to Learne to swimme vnlesse he bee giuen to Cramps and Convulsions; Howbeit I must confesse in my owne particular that I cannot swimme for as I was one tyme in Danger of Drowning by learning to swim my Mother vpon her blessing Charged mee neuer to learne swimming telling mee further That shee had heard of more drowned then saued by it, which reason though it did not prevaile with mee yet her Commandment did. It will bee good also for a Gentleman to learne to leape and wrastle and vault on horseback they being all of them Qualities of greate vse. I doe much approue likewise of shooting in the long bowe as being both an healthfull exercise and vsefull for the Warres Notwithstanding all that our Firemen speake against it; for bring 100 Archers against soe many Musketiers, I say If the Archer come within his distance hee will not only make two shootes but two hitts for one.

The Exercises I doe not approue of are Riding of running horses there being much Cheating in that kynde. Neither doe I see why a brave man should delight in a Creature whose cheife vse is to help him to run away: I doe not much like of hunting horses, that Exercise taking vp more tyme then can bee spared from a man studious to get knowledge. It is enough therefore to know the sport if there bee any in it without making it an ordinary practice And indeede of the two hawking is the better because lesse tyme is spent in it, And vpon those Termes also I can allow a litle bowling soe that the Company bee choice and good.

The Exercises I wholly Condemne are Dicing and Carding especially if you play for any greate summe of money or spend any tyme in them or vse to come to meetings in dicing houses where Cheaters meete to Cousen young men of all theire moneys; I could say much more concerning all these points of Education and particularly concerning That discreete Ciuillity which is to bee obserued in Communication either with freinds or strangers but that this worke would growe too bigg, And that many precepts conducing therevnto may bee had in Guazzo della Ciuile Conuersatione, and Galetaeus[1] de Moribus.

It will also deserue a particular Lecture or Recherche how one ought to behaue himselfe with his Children Neighbours Tennants and Servants, and I am Confident That precepts in this poynt will bee found more vsefull to young Gentlemen Then all the subtilityes of the schooles I confesse I haue collected many things to this purpose which I forbeare to set downe here because (If God graunt mee life and health) I intend to make a litle Treatise[2] concerning these poynts, I shall returne now to the Relation of my own History.

When I had attained the Age of about 18 and 19 yeares, My Mother together with my selfe and wife removed vp to London where wee tooke house and kept a greater Family then became either my Mothers widdows estate or such young beginners as wee were especially since six brothers and three sisters were to bee provided for, my Father having made either noe will or such an imperfect one that it was not proved: My Mother though shee had all my Fathers Leases[3] and goods which were of greate Ualue yet shee desired mee to vndertake that Burthen of providing for my brothers and sisters which to gratify my Mother as well as those soe neare mee I was voluntarily content to provide thus farre as to giue my six brothers thirty pounds a piece yearely during theire lives and my three sisters 1000 pounds a piece which portions married them to those I have abouementioned. My youngest sister[4] indeed might haue been married to a far greater fortune had not the Overthwartnes of some Neighbors interrupted it.

About the yeare of our Lord 1600 I came to London shortly after which the Attempt of the Earle of Essex[5] related in our History followed which I had rather were seene in the Writers of that Argument then here; Not long after This Curiosity rather then Ambition brought mee to Court And as it was the manner of those tymes for all men to kneele downe before the greate Queene Elizabeth, who then raigned, I was likewise vpon my knees in the Presence Chamber when shee passed by to the Chappell in whitehall. As soone as shee sawe mee shee stopt, and swearing her vsual Oath[1] demaunded who is this? Euery body theire present looked vpon mee but noe man knew mee till Sir James Croft a Pentioner[2] finding the Queene stayed returned back and tould who I was and that I had married Sir William Herberts of St. Gillians daughter; The Queene herevpon looked attentiuely vpon mee and swearing againe her Ordinary oath said, It is pitty he was married soe young and therevpon gaue mee her hand to kisse twice, both tymes gently Clapping mee on the Cheeke. I remember litle more of my self but that from that tyme vntill King James his coming to the Crowne, I had a sonne which died shortly afterwards and that I intended my studyes seriously, the more I learnt out of my bookes adding still a desire to knowe more.

King James being now acknowledgd King, and coming towards London I thought fitt to meete his Maiesty at Burley[3] neare Stanford; shortly after I was made Knight of the Bath with the vsual Seremonyes belonging to that Anncient Order,[4] wherevpon I could tell how much my person was commended by the Lords and Ladyes that came to see the Solemnitye then vsed but I shall flatter my selfe too much if I beleiued it.

I must not forget yet the Anncient Custome being that That some principall person was to put on the right Spurre of those the King had appointed to receiue that dignity. The Earle of Sherewsbury seeing my Esquire there with my Spurre in his hand the Earle of Sherewsbury voluntarily came to mee and said Cozen I beleiue you wilbee a good knight and therefore I will put on your spurr, wherevpon after my most humble thanks for soe great a favour I held vp my legg against the wall and he put on my Spurre.

There is another Custome likewise That the Knights the first day weare the Gowne of some religious order and the night following to bee bathed, After which they take an Oath neuer to sit in place where iniustice should bee done but they shall right it to the vttermost of their power and particularly Ladyes and Gentlewomen that shalbe wrongd in theire honor, if they demand Assistance, and many other Poynts not vnlike the Romances of Knights Errands.

The second day they are to weare Robes of Crimson Taffita (in which habit I am painted in my study)[1] and soe to ride from St. James to whitehall with our Esquires before vs and the third day to weare a gowne of purple sattin, vpon the left sleeue whereof is fastned certaine strings weaued of white silk and gould tyed in a Knott and Tassells to it of the same which all the Knights are obliged to weare vntill they haue done something famous in Armes or till some Lady of honor take it of and fasten it on her sleeue saying I will answer hee shall prove a good Knight. I had not long worne this string but a principall Lady of the Court and certainly in most mens opinion the handsommest[2] tooke mine of and said she would pledge her honor for myne; I doe not name this Lady because some passages hapned afterwards which oblige mee to silence though nothing could bee iustly said to her preiudice, or wrong.

Shortly after this I intended to goe with Charles Earle of Nottingham the Lord Admiral who went to Spaine[3] to take the Kings Oathe for the Confirmation of the Articles of Peace betwixt the two Crowns, howbeit by the Industry of some neare mee who desired to stay mee at Home I was hindred and instead of going that Uoyage was made Sheriffe of Mountgomeryshire, Concerning which I will say noe more but that I bestowed the Place of vnder shiriffe as also other places in my gifts freely without either taking money or reward, which Custome also I haue obserued throughout the wholle Course of my life In soe much That when I was Embassador in France I might have had greate presents which former Embassadors accepted of for doing lawfull Courtesies to Marchants and others yet noe Gratuity upon what Termes soeuer could euer bee fastned vpon mee.

This publique duty did not hinder mee yet to follow my beloved studyes in a Countrey life for the most part Though sometimes also I resorted to Court without yet that I had any Ambition there and much lesse was tainted with those Corrupt Delights incident to the Times, for living with my wife in all Coniugall Loyaltye for the space of about ten yeares after my Mariage I wholly declyned the Allurements and Temptations whatsoeuer which might inclyne mee to violat my mariag bed.

In the third yeare of King James The Gunpowder Treason hapening, My selfe who was Chosen Knight of the shire for Merionethshire as having resigned my Pretence in Mountgomeryshire to Sir William Herbert[1] at his entreaty did then lodg in my Mothers house neare Charing Crosse. The night before this horible Conspiracy was to bee acted I was two seuerall tymes warned in my sleepe not to goe to the Parliament that day which though I tooke but for dreaming fell out to bee an Admonition; For Sir Walter Cope coming the 5th of Nouember about six of the Clocke tould mee how the designe was discouered wishing mee not to goe out of my house vntill Businesses were better setled; Some few dayes after The Lords of the Counsell sent for mee And because the Conspirators were now in a Place in Staffordshire not far from Shropshire, They sent mee downe with Commission to Leavy forces to suppresse those who were in Arms against his Maiesty. Bcing now ready to goe Sir Thomas Dutton[2] offered his Company which I gladly accepted. Ryding Post thus wee came to Dudley in Staffordshire not far from a Place where the night before Conspirators by the falling of a sparke of fire vpon theire Gunpowder had theire faces burnt vpon which a notable mistake did happen. For Sir Thomas Dutton who had a fall by the way which had durtied his face being desirous to rest a while in the Inne to take the durt from his Clothes and to wash his face before wee came to Prestwood where wee intended to Lodg that night, wee allighted thus at an Inne there where the Maior with 20 or 30 naybers well weaponed cam in to vs And finding Sir Thomas Duttons face black on the one side imagined presently he was one of the Conspirators whom the Gunpowder had burnt, wherevpon also without informing himselfe further he justled Sir Thomas Dutton That hee almost threw him into the Fire. This Insolency made mee drawe my sword which Sir Thomas Dutton percieuing stept to mee telling mee in the Eare wee shall kill a dozen of them but wee should bee sure to bee killed our selues, Let me alone with this fellow. Sir Thomas Dutton then demanded why he justled him; he said, because he was a Traitor as might bee seene by the marks in his face; Sir Thomas Dutton replyed you shall see this mark quickly washed of and therevpon calling for water made cleane his Face. The maior was not yet satisfyed herewith but desired one to examine mee while he examined Sir Thomas Dutton. The Question he made to Sir Thomas Dutton was whence he came; he said from London. The Question demaunded of mee was whether wee went; I said to Staffordshire or Shropshire or wheresoeuer the Conspirators were, which a third person hearing said wee haue caught them in Contrary Tales already. Att which when wee had well laught The Maior with his Company retyred, and left vs to pursue our Iourney.

About the yeare 1608 My two daughters called Beatrice and Florance (who liued not long after) and one sonne Richard being borne and come to soe much maturity that though in their meere Childehood they gaue noe litle hopes of themselues for the future tyme, I called them all before my wife demanding how shee liked them? To which shee answering, Well, I demaunded then whether shee was willing to doe soe much for them as I would, wherevpon shee replying demaunded what I meant by that, I told her That for my part I was but young for a man and shee not old for a woman, that our Lifes were in the hands of God, That if he pleased to call either of vs away That Party which remained might marry againe and haue Children by some other to which our Estates might bee disposed; For preventing whereof I thought fitt to motion to her That if shee would assure vpon the sonnes any Quantity of Lands from 300 £ per annum to 1000 £ I would doe the like. But my wife not approving hereof answered in these expresse words That shee would not drawe the Cradle[1] vpon her hed, wherevpon I desiring her to advise better vpon the business and to take some few dayes respite for that purpose shee seemed to depart from mee not very well contented. About a weeke or ten dayes afterwards I demanded againe what shee thought concerning the motion I made, To which yet shee said noe more but that shee thought shee had already answered mee sufficiently to that poynt. I told her then That I should make another motion to her which was That in regard I was too young to goe beyond sea before I married her, shee now would giue mee leave for a while to see foraigne Countreys; Howbeit if shee would assure her lands as I would mine in the manner aboue-mentioned I would neuer depart from her, shee answered that I knew her minde before concerning that Poynt yet that shee should bee sorry I went beyond sea, neuertheles if I would needs goe shee could not help it. This, whether a License taken or giuen served my Turne to prepare without delay for a Iourney beyond sea That soe I might satisfy That Curiosity I long since had to see forraigne Countreys; soe that I might leaue my wife soe litle discontented as I could I left her not onely Posterity to renew the Family of the Herberts of St. Gillians according to her Father's desire to inherit his Lands but the Rents of all the Lands shee brought with her, re-serving my owne partly to pay by brothers and sisters Portions and defraying my charges abroad. Vpon which Termes though I was sorry to leaue my wife as having lived most loyally with her all this tyme I thought it noe iniust Ambition to attaine the Knowledge off Forraigne Countreys especially since I had in greate part already attained the Languages, and that I intended not to spend any long Time out of my Countrey.

Before I departed yet I left her with Childe of a Sonne Christned afterwards by the name of Edward. And now coming to Court I obtayned a License to goe Beyond sea taking with mee for my Companion Mr. Aurelian Townsend, a Gentleman That spake the Languages of Frensh Italian and Spanish, in greate Perfection and a man to waite in my Chamber who spake Frensh, two Lackyes and three horses; Coming thus to Dover and passing the seas thence to Callice I iorneyed without any memorable Aduenture till I came to Fauxbourg St. Germains[1] in Paris where Sir George Carue (then Ambassedour for the King) lived; I was kindely receiued by him and often invited to his table. Next to his house dwelt the Duke of Uantadour who had maried a daughter of Monsieur de Montmorency

Grand Conestable de France. Many visits being exchanged betweene that Dutches and the Lady of our Ambassedour It pleased the Dutches to invite mee to her Father's house at the Castle of Merlou¹ being about 24 miles from Paris; And here I found much wellcome from that brave ould Generall, who being informed of my names said he knew well of what Family I was, telling vs the first notice he had of the Herberts was at the Siege of St. Quintence where my Grandfather with a Command of Foote vnder William Earle of Penbrooke was. Passing two or three dayes here It hapned one Evening that a daughter of the Dutches of about ten or eleuen yeares of Age, going from the Castle to walke in the meadows, My selfe with diuers Frensh Gentlemen attended her and some Gentlewomen that were with her; This young Lady wearing a knot of Reband² on her head A Frensh Cavelier tooke it of suddainlye and fastned it to his hatband; The young Lady offended herewith demaunds her Reband But he refusing to restore it the young Lady addressing her selfe to mee said Monsieur I pray you get my Reband from that Gentleman; Herevpon going towards him I courteously with my hatt in my hand desired him to doe mee the honor That I might deliuer the Lady her Reband or Bouquet againe, But he roughly answering mee, doe you thinke I will giue it you when I haue refused it to her? I replyed Nay then Sir I will make you restore it by Force, wherevpon also putting on my hat and reaching att his he to saue himselfe run away and after a long Course in the meadow finding That I had almost ouertooke him he turned short and running to the young Lady was about to put the Reband in her hand when I seasing vpon his Arme said to the young Lady It was I that gaue it you. Pardon mee, quoth she It is hee that giues it mee; I said then, Madam I will not contradict you But if hee dare say That I did not constraine him to giue it you, I will fight with him. The Frensh Gentleman answered nothing therevnto for the present, and soe I conducted the young Lady againe to the Castle; The next day I desired Mr. Aurelian Townsend to tell the Frensh Cauellier, That either hee must confesse That I constrayned him to restore the Reband or fight with mee, But the Gentleman seeming vnwilling to

accept this Challenge, went out from the place, wherevpon I following him some of the Gentlemen that belonged to the Conestable
taking notice hereof acquainted him therewith, who sending for the
Frensh Cauelier checked him well for his Sawcynesse in taking the
Reband away from his Grandchild and afterwards bid him depart
his house; And this was all that euer I heard of the Gentleman,
with whome I proceeded in that manner because I thought my selfe
obliged therevnto by the oath taken when I was made Knight of the
Bath as I formerly related.

Vpon this Occasion I must remember also that vpon the same
poynt three other times I engaged my selfe to Challenge men to
fight with mee who I conceiued had Iniured Ladyes and Gentlewomen, One was in defence of my Cozen Sir Francis Newports
daughter, who was married to John Barker of Hamon; A younger
brother and heir to the said John Barker called Walter Barker having
betrayed my Cozen who though shee vsing perchance more liberty
then became her with a servant in the house whome shee favoured
aboue the rest, Walter Barker as I was tould by others nourished the
said familiarity and afterwards discouered it to his Brother which
part of his being Treacherous (as I conceiued it) I thought fitt to
send him a challenge which to this day hee neuer Answered and
would haue beaten him afterwards but that I was hindred by my
Vnkle Sir Francis Newport.

I had another Occasion to Challeng one Captain Uaughan[1] who I
conceiued offered some Iniury to my sister The Lady Jones of
Abermarlas: I sent him a Challeng which hee accepted The place
betweene vs being appointed beyond Greenewich with seconds on
both sides; Herevpon I coming to the King's head in Greenwich
with Intention the next morning to bee in the Place, I found the
house besett with at least 100 persons partly sent by the Lords of the
privy Counsell, who gaue order to apprehend mee. I hearing thereof
desired my servant to bring my horses as farr as he could from my
Lodging, but yet within sight of mee which being done and all the
Company coming to lay hould on mee, I and my second who was
my Cozen James Price of Vanachly[2] sallied out of the Doores with

our swords drawne and in spight of that multitude made our way to our horses where my servant very honestly opposing himselfe against those who would haue layd hands vpon vs, while wee got vp on horseback was himselfe laid holt on by them, and euil treated, which I seeing ryd back againe and with my sword in my hand rescued him; And afterwards seeing him get on horsebacke charged them to goe any where rather then to follow mee; ryding afterwards with my second to the Place appointed I found noe body there which as I heard afterwards happned because the Lords of the Counsell taking notice of this Difference apprehended him and Charged him in his Maiestyes name not to fight with mee, since otherwise I beleiue hee would not haue failed.

The third that I questioned in this kynde was a Scotch Gentleman[1] who taking a Reband in the like manner from Mrs. Middlemore a Maid of honor, as he did from the young Lady abouementioned, in a back Roome behinde Queene Annes Lodgings in Greenwich, shee likewise desired mee to get her the said Reband. I repaired as formerly to him in a Courteous manner to demaund it, But he refusing as the Frensh Cauelier did I caught him by the Neck and had almost throwne him downe, when Company came in and parted vs, I offered likewise to fight with this gentleman and came to the Place appointed by Hide Park but this also was Interrupted by order of the Lords of the Counsell, and I neuer heard more of him.

These Passages though different in time I haue related here together both for the similitude of Argument, and that it may appeare how strictly I held my selfe to my Oath of Knighthood. For the rest I can truly say That though I haue lived in the Armyes and Courts of the greatest Princes in Christendome yet I neuer had quarrell with man for my owne sake, noe not although in my owne Nature I was euer Chollerique and hasty yet I neuer without occasion quarrelled with any body. And as litle did any body attempt to giue mee offence as having as cleare a Reputation for my Courage as whosoeuer of my Time. For my freinds often I haue hazzarded my self but neuer had occasion to drawe my sword for my owne sake, as hating euer the doing of Iniury and contenting my selfe onely to resent them when they were offered mee; After this digression I shall returne to my History in France.

That Braue Conestable de France testifying now more than formerly his regard of mee at his departure from Merlou to his faire house att Chantilly[1] fiue or six mile distant said he left that Castle to bee Commanded by mee, As also his Forrests and Chaces which were well stored with wilde bore and stagg, and that I might hunt them when I pleased. He tould mee also that if I would learne to ride the greate horse hee had a stable there of some fifty the best and Choicest as was thought in France And that his Escuyer called Monsieur de Disanqur not inferior to Pluvenel or La-brove should teach mee. I did with much thankfullnes accept his Offer as being very much addicted to the Exercise of riding greate horses: And as for hunting in his Forrests I tould him I should vse it sparingly as being desirous to preserue his Game. Hee commanded also his Escuyer to keepe a Table for mee, and his Pages to attend mee The cheife of whom was Monsieur de Mennon[2] who proving to bee one of the best horsemen in France keepes now an Academy in Paris. And here I shall recount a litle Passage betwixt him and his Master, That the Inclination of the Frensh at that tyme may appeare, there being scarce any man thought worthy the looking on that had not killed some other in Duel: Mennon desiring to mary a Neece of Monsieur Disanqur who it was thought should bee his heire was thus answered by him, Freind it is not tyme yet to marry. I will tell you what you must doe if you will bee a brave man; you must first kill in single Combate two or three men, then afterwards marry and ingender two or three Children, or the World had neuer got nor lost by you; Of which strange Counsell Disanqur was noe otherwise an Author then as he had been an exaumple, It being his fortune to haue fought 3 or foure braue duells in his tyme.

And now as euery morning I mounted the Greate horse soe in the Afternoones I many times went a hunting The manner of which was thus, The Duke of Montmorency having giuen order to the Tennants of the Towne of Merlou and some villages adioyning to attend mee when I went a hunting; They vpon my summons vsually repaired to those woods where I intended to finde my Game with Drumms and Musketts to the number of sixty or eighty and sometimes one hundred or more persons, they entring the wood on the one side with much Noyse discharging theire pieces and beating theire drumms, wee on the other side of the said wood having placed mastiffes and Grayhounds to the number of twenty or thirty which Monsieur de Montmorency kept neare his Castle, expected those beasts they should force out of the woods; If staggs or wilde bores came forth wee comonly spared them Pursuing onely the wolves which were there in greate number, Of which wee found two sorts: The Mastiffe woolfe thick and short though hee could not indeede run fast, yet would fight cruelly with our Doggs; The Greyhound woolfe long and swift, many tymes escaped our best doggs, though when overtaken was easily killed by vs, without making much resistance; Of both these sorts I killed diuers with my sword while I stayed there.

One tyme also It was my Fortune to kill a wilde bore in this manner: The boar being rowsed from his Denne fled before our doggs for a good space but finding them presse him hard turnd head against them, and had now hurt three or fowre of them very dangerously when I came on horseback vp to him and with my sword thrust him twice or thrice without yet that I could enter his skinne, the blade being not soe stiffe as it could perce him; The Bore herevpon turned vpon mee and much indangered my horse which I perceiuing rid a little out of the way and leaving my horse with my Lacky returned on foote with my sword against the Bore who by this tyme had hurt more doggs and here happned a pretty kinde of fight for when I thrust at the Bore sometimes with my sword which in some places I made enter the Bore would run at mee whose Tusks yet by stepping a litle out of the way I avoyded, But he then turning vpon mee the doggs came in and drew him of, soe that he fell vpon them, which I perceiving ran at the Boare with my sword againe, which made him charge mee, but then the doggs pulled him from mee againe while soe relieving one another by

Turns wee killed the Bore. At this Chace Monsieur Disanqur and Mennon were present as also Mr. Townsend yet soe as they did endeavour rather to withdrawe mee from then Assist mee in the danger. Of which Bore some part being well seasoned and Larded, I sent to my Vnkle Francis Newport in Shropshire, who found it most excellent meate.

And Thus I past a wholle Summer partly in these exercises and partly in Uisitts of the Duke of Montmorency at his faire house in Chantilly, which for its extraordinary fairnes and scituation I shall here describe: A litle River descending from some higher grounds in a Countrey which was almost all his owne and falling at Last vpon a Rock in the middle of a Ualley which to keepe its way forwards must on one or other side thereof haue declyned its Course. Some of the Ancestors of the Montmorencyes to ease the River of this Labour made diuers Channells through this Rock to giue it free passage, dividing the Rocke by that meanes into little Islands vpon which he built a greate and strong Castle, ioyned together with Bridges and sumptuously founded[1] with hangings of silke and gould, rare Pictures and Statues, All which Buildings vnited as I formerly tould were incompassed about with water, which was paved with Stone (those which were vsed in the building of the House being drawne from thence). One might see the huge Carps Pikes and Trouts which were kept in seurall Divisions glyding along the waters very easily, yet in my opinion nothing added soe much to the Glory of this Castle as a Forest adioyning close to it, and vpon a levell with the house, for being of a very large extent and sett thick both with tall trees and vnderwoods the wholle Forrest which was replenished with wilde Bore Stagg and Rowe was cutt out into Long walks euery way, soe that although the doggs might follow theire Chace through the Thicketts, the Huntsmen might ride along the said walks and meete theire Game in some one of them, as being Cutt with that Art that they led to all the parts in the said Forrest and here also I haue hunted the wilde Bore diuers tymes: Both then and afterwards when his sonne the Duke of Montmorency succeeded him in that incomparable place.

47

And here I cannot but remember the direction the old Conestable gaue mee to returne to his Castle out of this Admirable Laborinth telling mee I should looke vpon what side the trees were roughest and hardest which being found I might bee Confident that part stood northward which being obserued I might easily finde the East as being on the right hand and soe guide my way home.

How much this house together with the Forrest hath beene valued by Greate Princes, may appeare by two little Narratives I shall here insert: Charles the fifth the Greate Emperour passing in the tyme of Fransoy the first from Spayne into the Lowe Countreys by the way of France was entertayned, for sometyme in this House, By a Duke of Momorentcy who was likewise Coonestable de France; After he had taken this Pallace into his Consideration with the Forrest adioyning said he would willingly giue one of his Provinces in the Lowe Countreys for such a place, there being as he thought no where such a Scituation.

Henery the fourth also was desirous of this house and offered to Exchange any of his houses with much more lands then his Estate thereabouts was worth, To which the Duke of Momorency made this wary answer: *Sire, la maison est a vous mais quae sois le concierge* which in English sounds thus: Sir, the house is yours but giue me leaue to keepe it for you.

When I had been at Merlou about some eight moneths and attained as was thought the Knowledg of horsemanship I came to the Duke of Momorency at Chantily, and after due thanks for his favours tooke my leave of him to goe to Paris, wherevpon the good old Prince embraceing mee and calling me, Sonne bid mee farewell assuring mee neuerthelesse hee should bee glad of any Occasion hereafter to testify his Love and Esteeme for mee telling mee further hee should come to Paris himselfe shortly where he hoped to see mee; from hence I returned to Merlou where I gaue Monsieur Disanqur such a present as abundantly requited the Charges of my diet and the Paines of his teaching: Being now ready to set forth A Gentleman from the Duke of Montmorency came to mee and told mee his Master would not let mee goe without giving mee a present which

I might keepe as an earnest of his Affection: wherevpon also a Genet for which the Duke had sent expressly into Spaine and which cost him there 500 Crownes as I was tould was brought mee. The Greatnes of this Gift together with other Courtesies receiued did litle[1] trouble mee as not knowing then how to requite them. I would haue given my horses I had there which were of greate Ualue backe to him But that I thought them too meane a present, But the duke also suspecting that I meant to doe soe prevented mee, saying That as I loved him I should thinke vpon noe requitall while I stayd in France, But when I came into England if I sent him a Mare that ambled naturally I should much gratify him; I tould the Messinger I should striue both that way and euery way els to declare my thankfullnes and soe dismist the Messinger with a good reward.

Coming now to Paris through the Recommendation of the Lord Ambassador I was lodged in the house of that Incomparable scholler, Isaak Cawsabon by whose learned Conversation I much benefited my selfe besides I did apply my selfe much to knowe the vse of my Armes and to ride the greate horse, Playing on the Lute and singing according to the Rules of the Frensh Masters.

Sometimes also I went to the Court of the Frensh King Henry the fourth, who vpon Information of mee in the Garden of the Tuileries receiued mee with all Courtesie embraceing mee in his Armes and holding mee some while there. I went sometimes also to the Court of Queene Margaret[2] at the hostel called by her name, And here I sawe many Balls or Masks, In all which It pleased that Queene publiquely to place mee next to her Cheare not without the wonder of some and the envy of another who was wont to have that favor; I shall recount one accident which happened while I was there.

All things being ready for the Ball, and every one being in their place, and I my self next to the Queen, expecting when the Dancers would come in, One knockt at the Door somewhat lowder than became, as I thought, a very civil Person; when he came in, I remember there was a suddain whisper among the Ladies, saying C'est Monsieur Balagny, or 'tis Monsieur Balagny, whereupon also

I saw the Ladies and Gentlewomen one after another invite him to sit near them, and which is more, when one Lady had his company a while, another would say, you have injoyed him long enough I must have him now, at which bold Civility of theirs, though I were astonished, yet it added unto my wonder, that his Person could not be thought at most but ordinary handsome; his hair which was cut very short, half gray, his doublet but of Sackcloth cut to his shirt, and his breeches only of plain gray cloth; informing my self by some standers by who He was, I was told that he was one of the Gallantest Men in the World as having killed eight or nine men in single fight, and that for this reason the Ladies made so much of him, it being the manner of all French women to cherish Gallant men, as thinking they could not make so much of any else with the safety of their honor. This Cavelier though his head was half grey, he had not yet attained the Age of thirty years, whom I have thought fit to remember more particularly here because of some passages that happened afterwards betwixt him and me, at the Siege of Julires as I shall tell in its Place.

Having past thus all the winter untill about the latter End of January[1] without any such memorable accident as I shall think fitt to set down particularly, I took my Leave of the French King, Queen Margaret, and the Nobles and Ladies in both Courts; At which time the Princess of Conti desired me to carry a Scarf into England, and present it to Queen Ann on her part, which being accepted, my Self and Sir Thomas Lucy (whose second I had been twice in France against two Caveliers of our Nation, who yet were hindred to fight with us in the field, where we attended them) We came on our way as far as Diep in Normandy, and there took ship about the beginning of February, when so furious a storm arose, that with very great danger we were at Sea all night, the Master of our Ship lost both the use of his Compas and his reason, for not knowing whither he was carried by the tempest, all the help he had was by the lightnings, which together with Thunder very frequently that night terrified him, yet gave the advantage sometimes to discover whether we were upon our Coast, to which he thought by the course of his glasses we were near approached; and now towards day we found our selfes by great providence of God within View of Dover, to which the Master of our Ship did make: The men at Dover rising by times in the morning to see whether any ship were coming towards them, were in great numbers upon the shoar, as believing that tempest which had thrown down Barns and Trees near the Town, might give them the benefit of some Wrack, if perchance any ship were driven thitherwards; we coming thus in extream danger straight upon the Peer of Dover which stands out in the Sea, our ship was unfortunately split against it; the Master said, mes Amies nous sommes perdus, or my Friends we are cast away, when my selfe who heard the ship crack against the Peer, and then found by the Masters words it was time for every one to save themselves, if they could, got out of my Cabin (though very seasick) and climing up the mast a litle way, drew my sword and flourished it; they at Dover having this signe given them, adventured in a Shallop of six Oars to relieve us, which being come with great danger to the side of our Ship, I got into it first with my sword in my hand, and called for Sir Thomas Lucy, saying that if any man offer'd to get in before him, I should resist him with my sword, whereupon a faithfull servant of his taking Sir Thomas Lucy out of the Cabin, who was half dead of Seasicknes, put him into my Arms, whom after I had receiv'd, bid the Shalop make away to shoar, and the rather that I saw another Shalop coming to relieve us; When a post from France who carried Letters finding the ship still rent more and more, adventured to leap from the top of our ship into the Shalop, where falling fortunately on some of the stronger Tymber of the Boat and not of the Planks, which he must needs have broken, and so sunk us, had he fallen upon them, escaped together with us two, unto the Land; I must confess my self as also the Seamen that were in the Shalop thought once to have killed him for this desperate attempt, but finding no harm followed, We escaped together unto the Land, from whence we sent more Shalops, and so made means to save both men and horses that were in the Ship, which yet it self was wholy split and cast away, insomuch that in pity to the Master,

Sir Thomas Lucy and my self gave thirty pounds towards his Loss, which yet was not so great as we thought, since the Tide now ebbing he recover'd the broken parts of his ship.

Coming thus to London and afterwards to Court, I kissed his Majesties hand, and acquainted him with some particulars concerning France. As for the Present I had to deliver to her Majesty from the Princess of Conty, I thought fit rather to send it by One of the Ladies that attended her than to presume to demand audience of her in Person: but her Majesty not satisfied herewith commanded me to attend her, and demanded divers questions of me concerning that Princess and the Courts in France, saying She would speak more at large with me at some other time, for which purpose She commanded me to wait on her often, wishing me to advise her what Present she might return back again.

Howbeit not many weeks after I return'd to my Wife and Family againe where I passed some time, partly in my Studies and partly riding the great horse, of which I had a stable well furnish'd; no horse yet was so dear to me as the Genet, I brought from France, whose Love I had so gotten that he would suffer none else to ride him, nor indeed any man to come near him, when I was upon him as being in his nature a most furious horse; his true Picture may be seen in the Chappel Chamber in my house where I am painted riding him, and this Motto by me,

> Me totum Bonitas bonum suprema
> Reddas; me intrepidum dabo vel ipse.[1]

This horse as soon as ever I came to the stable would neigh, and when I drew nearer him, would lick my hand, and (when I suffer'd him) my cheek, but yet would permit nobody to come near his heels at the same time; Sir Thomas Lucy would have given me 200 l. for this horse, which though I would not accept, yet I left the horse with him when I went to the Low-Countrys, who not long after died; the occasion of my going thither was thus, hearing that a War[2] about the Title of Cleave, Juliers and some other Provinces betwixt the Low-Countrys and Germany should be made by

Edward, Lord Herbert of Cherbury; oil painting attributed to W. Larkin

*James I; oil
painting by
P. van Somers*

*Anne of
Denmark; oil
painting by
P. van Somers*

the several Pretenders to it, and that the French King himself would come with a great Army unto those Parts. It was now the year of our Lord 1610 when my Lord Shandois and myself resolved to take Shipping for the Low Countrys, and from thence to pass to the City of Juliers, which she Prince of Orange resolved to besiege; making all hast thither we found the siege newly begun; the Low Country Army assisted by 4000 English under the command of Sir Edward Cecill. We had not been long there, when the Mareshall de Chartres instead of Henry the 4th who was killed by that Villain Ravalliac came with a brave French Army thither. In which Monsieur Balagny I formerly mention'd was a Collonel.

My Lord Shandois lodging himself in the Quarters where Sir Horace Vere was, I went and quarter'd with Sir Edward Cecill, where I was lodged next to him in a hutt I made there, going yet both by day and night to the Trenches, We making our Approaches to the Town on the one side and the French on the other. Our Lines were drawn towards the point of a Bulwark of the Cittadel or Castle, thought to be one of the best fortifications in Christiandome, and incompassed about with a deep wet ditch, we lost many men in making these approaches, the Town and Castle being very well provided both with great and smal shot, and a Garrison in it of about 4000 men besides the Burghers; Sir Edward Cecill (who was a very active General) used often during this Siege to go in person in the night time to try whether he could catch any Sentinells perdues;[1] and for this purpose still desir'd me to accompany him, in performing whereof both of us did much hazard our selves, for the first Sentinell retiring to the second, and the second to the third, three shots were commonly made at us before we could do anything, though afterwards chacing them with our swords almost home unto their Guards we had some sport in the pursuite of them.

One day Sir Edward Cecill and my self coming to the approaches that Monsieur de Balagny had made towards a Bullwark or Bastion of that City, Monsieur de Balagny in the presence of Sir Edward Cecill and diverse English and French Captains then present, said, Monsieur, On dit, que vous êtes un des plus braves de vôtre Nation, et Je suis Balagny, allons voir qui faira le meius, They say, you are one of the bravest of your Nation, and I am Balagny, let us see who will do best; whereupon leaping suddainly out of the Trenches with his sword drawn, I did in the like manner as suddainly follow him, both of us in the mean while striving who should be foremost, which being perceiv'd by those of the Bullwark and Cortine[1] opposite to us, three or four hundred shot at least great and smal were made against us. Our running on forwards in Emulation of each other was the cause that all the shots fell betwixt us and the Trench from which we sallied. When Monsieur Balagny finding such a storm of Bullets, said, par Dieu il fait bien chaud, it is very hot here; I answer'd briefly thus, vous en ires primier, autrement Je n'iray jamais, You shall go first or else I will never go, hereupon he ran with all speed, and somewhat crouching towards the Trenches, I followed after leasurely and upright, and yet came within the Trenches before they on the Bullwark or Cortine could charge again,[2] which passage afterwards being related to the Prince of Orange, he said it was a strange Bravado of Balagny, and that we went to an unavoydable death.

I could relate diverse things of Note concerning my self, during the Siege, but do forbear, least I should relish too much of Vanity; it shall suffise that my passing over the Ditch unto the Wall first of all the Nations there, is set down by William Crosse[3] master of Arts and Souldier, who hath written and printed the History of the Low-Countrys.

There hapned during this Siege a particular Quarrel[4] betwixt me and the Lord of Walden, Eldest Son to the Earle of Suffolk, Lord Treasurer of England at that time, which I do but unwillingly relate in regard of the great esteem I have of that Noble Family, howbeit to avoid misreports I have thought fit to set it down truly, that Lord having been invited to a Feast in Sir Horace Vere's quarters, where (after the Low Country manner) there was liberal drinking, returned not long after to Sir Edward Cecil's quarters, at which time I speaking merrily to him upon some slight occasion, he took that offence at me which he would not have done at another time, insomuch that he came towards me in a violent manner, which I perceiving did more than half way meet him; But the Company were so vigilant upon us that before any blow past we were separated; howbeit because he made towards me, I thought fit the next day to send him a Challenge, telling him that if he had any thing to say to me, I would meet him in such a place as no man should interrupt us: shortly after this Sir Thomas Payton came to me on his part, and told me, my Lord would fight with me on horseback with single sword, and said he I will be his Second, where is yours? I replied that neither his Lordship nor my self brought over any great Horses with us; that I knew he might much better borrow one than my Self; howbeit as soon as he shewed me the place, he should find me there on horseback or on foot; whereupon both of us riding together upon two Geldings to the side of a Wood, Payton said he chose that place, and the time break of day the next morning; I told him I would fail neither place nor time, though I knew not where to get a better horse than the Nag I rid on, and as for a Second I shall trust to your nobleness, who I know will see fair play betwixt us, though you come on his side. But he urging me again to provide a Second, I told him I could promise for none but my Self, and that if I spoke to any of my friends in the Army to this purpose, I doubted least the business might be discover'd and prevented.

He was no sooner gone from me, but night drew on, my self resolving in the mean time to rest under a fair Oak all night; after this, tying my horse by the bridle unto another Tree, I had not now rested two hours when I found some fires nearer to me than I thought was possible in so solitary a place, whereupon also having the curiosity to see the reason hereof, I got on horse back again, and had not rode very far when by the talk of the Souldiers there, I found I was in the Scotch Quarter, where finding in a stable a very fair horse of service, I desired to know whether he might be bought for any reasonable Sum of money, but a souldier replying it was their Captains, Sir Iames Areskin's[1] chief horse, I demanded for Sir Iames, but the souldier answering he was not within the Quarter, I demanded then for his Lieutenant, whereupon the Souldier courteously desired him to come to me, this Lieutenant was called Montgomery, and had the reputation of a gallant man, I told him that I would very fain buy a horse, and if it were possible, the horse I saw but a litle before, but he telling me none was to be sold there, I offer'd to leave in his hands 100 pieces if he would lend me a good horse for a day or two, he to restore me the money again when I deliver'd him the horse in good plight, and did besides bring him some present as a gratuity.

The Lieutenant though he did not know me, suspected I had some private quarrel, and that I desired this horse to fight on, and thereupon told me, Sir, whosoever you are, you seem to be a person of worth, and you shall have the best horse in the stable, and if you have a Quarrel and want a Second, I offer my self to serve you upon another horse, and if you will let me go along with you upon these terms, I will ask no pawn of you for the horse. I told him I woud use no Second, and I desired him to accept 100 pieces which I had there about me in pawn for the horse, and he shoud here from me shortly again, and that though I did not take his noble offer of coming along with me, I shoud evermore rest much obliged to him, whereupon giving him my purse with the money in it, I got upon his horse and left my Nagg besides with him.

Riding thus away about twelve a clock at night to the wood from whence I came, I alighted from my horse and rested there 'till morning, the day now breaking I got on horse back and attended the Lord of Walden with his Second. The first person that appeared was a footman, who I heard afterwards was sent by the Lady of Walden, who as soon as he saw me, ran back again with all speed; I meant once to pursue him, but that I thought it better at last to keep my place. About two hours after Sir William St. Leiger now Lord President of Munster came to me, and told me he knew the cause of my being there, and that the business was discover'd by the Lord Walden's rising so early that morning, and the suspicion that he meant to fight with me, and had Sir Thomas Payton with him, and that he would ride to him, and that there were 30 or 40 sent after us, to hinder us from meeting, shortly after many more came to the

Place where I was, and told me I must not fight, and that they were sent for the same purpose, and that it was to no purpose to stay there, and thence rode to seek the Lord of Walden; I stayed yet two hours longer, but finding still more company came in, rode back again to the Scotch Quarters, and deliver'd the horse back again, and receiv'd my money and Nag from Lieutenant Montgomery, and so withdrew my self to the French Quarters, 'till I did find some convenient time to send againe to the Lord Walden.

Being among the French I remembered my self of the Bravado of Monsieur Balagny, and coming to him told him, I knew how brave a man he was, and that as he had put me to one tryall of daring when I was last with him in his Trenches I would put him to another, saying I heard he had a fair Mistriss, and that the Scarf he wore was her gift, and that I would maintain I had a worthier Mistriss than he, and that I would do as much for her sake as he or any else durst do for his; Balagny hereupon looking merrily upon me, said, if we shall try who is the abler man to serve his Mistriss, let both of us get two Wenches, and he that doth his business best, let him be the braver man; and that for his part, he had no mind to fight on that Quarrell; I looking hereupon somewhat disdainfully on him, said he spoke more like a Paillard[1] than a Cavelier, to which he answering nothing I rid my wayes, and afterwards went to Monsieur Terant a French Gentleman that belonged to the Duke of Montmorency formerly mention'd, who telling me he had a Quarrel with another Gentleman, I offered to be his Second, but he saying he was provided already, I rode thence to the English Quarters, attending some fitt occasion to send againe to the Lord Walden; I came no sooner thither, but I found Sir Thomas Sommerset with 11 or 12 more in the head of the English, who were then drawing forth in a Body or Squadron, who seeing me on horseback with a footman only that attended me, gave me some affronting words for my Quarrelling with the Lord of Walden, whereupon I alighted and giving my horse to my Lacky, drew my sword, which he no sooner saw but he drew his, as also all the Company with him, I running hereupon amongst them, put by some of their Thrusts, and making towards him in particular put by a Thrust of his, and had certainly run him through, but that one Lieutenant Prichard at that instant taking me by the shoulder turned me aside, but I recovering my self again ran at him a second time, which he perceiving retired himself with the Company to the Tents which were near, though not so fast but I hurt one Proger and some others also that were with him; but they being all at last got within the Tents, I finding now nothing else to be done, got to my horse again, having receiv'd only a slight hurt on the outside of my Ribbs, and two Thrusts, the one through the skirts of my Doublet, and the other through my breeches, and about 18 nicks upon my sword and hilt, and so rode to the Trenches before Iulies, where our Souldiers were.

Not long after this the Town being now surrendered,[1] and every body preparing to go their ways, I sent again a Gentleman to the Lord of Walden to offer him the meeting with my sword, but this was avoided not very handsomely by him (contrary to what Sir Henry Rich now Earle of Holland, perswaded him.)

After having taken leave of his Excellency Sir Edward Cecill, I thought fit to return on my way homewards as far as Dusseldorp, I had been scarce two hours in my Lodgings when one Lieutenant Hamilton brought a Letter from Sir Iames Areskin (who was then in Town likewise) unto me, the effect whereof was, that in regard his Lieutenant Montgomery had told him that I had the said Iames Areskins consent for borrowing his Horse, he did desire me to do one of two things which was either to disavow the said words, which he thought in his conscience I never spake, or if I would justifie them, then to appoint time and place to fight with him; having considered a while what I was to do in this case, I told Lieutenant Hamilton that I thought my selfe bound in honor to accept the most noble part of his Proposition which was to fight with him, when yet perchance it might bee easily enough for mee to say That I had his horse vpon other Termes then was affirmed where-vpon also giving Lievetenant Hamelton the length of my sword I told him that as soone as euer he had matcht it I would fight with him wishing him further to make haste, since I desired to end the busines as speedily as could bee, Lievetenant Hamilton herevpon returning back mett in a crosse streete (I know not by what miraculous Aduenture) Lieuetenant Mountgomery Conveying diuers of the hurt and maymed souldiers at the seige of St. Julias vnto that Towne to bee lodged and drest by the Chirurgions there; Hamilton herevpon calling to Mountgomery tould him the effect of his Captains letter together with my Answer. Montgomery noe sooner heard this but he replyed (as Hamilton told mee afterwards) I see that Noble Gentleman chooseth rather to fight then to Contradict mee, but my telling a Lye must not bee an occasion why either my Captain or hee should hazard theire lifes. I will alight from my horse and tell my Captain presently how all that matter past, wherevpon also hee related the busines about borrowing the horse in that manner I formerly set downe which as soone as Sir James Areskins heard he sent Lieutenant Hamilton to mee presently againe to tell mee hee was satisfyed how the busines past and that he had nothing to say to mee but that hee was my most humble servant and was sorry he euer questioned mee in that manner.

Some occasions detayning mee in Dusseldorp the next day Lievetenant Mountgomery came to mee, and told mee he was in danger of loosing his Place and desired mee to make meanes, to his Excellency the Prince of Aurenge That hee might not bee Cashired or els that hee was vndone; I tould him that either I would keepe him in his place or take him as my Companion and freind and allow him sufficient meanes till I could provide him another place as good as it, which he taking very kindly but desiring cheifly he might goe with my Letter to the Prince of Aurenge I obtained at last he should bee restored to his place againe.

And now taking boate I past along the Ryver of Rine to the Lowe-Countreys where after some stay I went to Antwerp and Bruxells and having stayd a while in the Court there, went from thence to Callice where taking ship I arriued at Dover and soe went to London; I had scarce beene two dayes there when the Lords of the Counsell sending for mee ended the difference betwixt My Lord of Walden and my selfe. And now if I may say it without vanity, I was in greate Esteeme both in Court and Citty, many of the greatest desiring my Company though yet before that tyme I had noe acquaintance with them: Richard Earle of Dorset to whom otherwise I was a stranger one day invited mee to Dorset House[1], where bringing mee into his Gallery and shewing mee many Pictures hee at last brought mee to a Frame covered with greene Taffita and asked mee who I thought was there and therewithall presently drawing the Courtaine shewed mee my owne Picture wherevpon demaunding how his Lordship came to haue it, hee answered That he had heard soe many brave things of mee, That he gott a Coppy of a Picture[2] which one Larkin a Painter drew for mee, The Originall whereof I intended before my departure to the Low Countrey for Sir Thomas Lucy. But not onely the Earle of Dorset but a greater person[3] then I will here nominat, got another Coppy from Larkin and placing it after in her Cabinet (without that euer I knew any such thing was done) gaue occasion to those who sawe it after her death of more discourse then I could haue wisht, And indeed I may truly say that taking of my Picture was fatall to mee for more reason than I shall think fitt to deliuer.

There was a Lady also wife to Sir John Aeres, Knight who finding some meanes to get a Copy did afterwards get it contracted in to a litle forme by Isaac the Painter according to his manner and afterwards, caused it to bee set in gould and Enamiled and soe wore it about her neck soe lowe that shee yet hid it vnder her brests, which I conceiue coming afterwards to the knowledg of Sir John Aeres gaue him more cause of Iealousie then needed had he knowne how Innocent I was from pretending to any thing which might wrong him or his Lady since I could not soe much as imagine that euer shee had my Picture or that shee did beare more then ordinary Affection to mee. It is true that as shee had place in Court and attended on Queene Anne, and was beside of an excellent witt and discourse shee had made her selfe a Considerable person, Howbeit litle more then common Ciuility euer past betwixt vs, Though I confesse no man was wellcomer to her when I came for which I shall alledge this Passage:

Coming one daye into her Chamber I sawe her through the
Courtaines lying vpon her bed with a wax Candle in one hand and
the Picture I formerly mentioned in the other. I coming therevpon
somewhat boldly to her shee blew out the Candle and hid the
Picture from mee; My selfe therevpon being Curious to know
what that was shee held in her hand got the Candle to bee lighted
againe, by means whereof I found it was my Picture shee looked
vpon with more earnestnesse and Passion than I could haue easily
beleiued especially since my selfe was not ingaged in any affection
towards her. I could willingly haue omitted this Passage but that it
was the begining of a bloody history which followed howsoeuer yet
I must before the eternal God cleare her honor. And now in Court a
greate Person[1] sent for mee diuers tymes to attend her, which
summons though I obeyed yet (God knoweth) I declyned coming
to her as much as conveniently I could, without Incurring her dis-
pleasure and this I did not onely for very honest reasons but to speake
Ingeniously because that Affection past betwixt mee and some other
Lady who I belieue was the fairest of the tyme as nothing could
diuert it. I had not beene long in London when a violent burning
Fever seased vpon mee, which brought mee almost to my death
Though at last I did by slowe degrees recouer my health; being thus
vpon my Amendment my Lord Lisle afterwards Earle of Leicester
sent mee word that Sir John Aers intended to kill mee in my Bed
and wisht mee to keepe a Guard vpon my Chamber and Person,
the same Aduertisement was confirmed by Lucie Countes of Bedford, and the Lady Hobby shortly after. Hereupon I thought fitt
to intreat Sir William Herbert now Lord Powis to goe to Sir John
Aeres and tell him That I maruelled much at the Information given
mee by these greate Persons. And that I could not imagine any
sufficient ground thereof Howbeit if hee had any thing to say to
mee in a faire and noble way I would giue him the meeting as soone
as I had got strength enough to stand vpon my Leggs: Sir William
herevpon brought mee soe ambiguous and doubtfull an answer from
him that whatsoeuer he meant he listed not to declare yet his Intention which was really as I found afterwards to kill mee any way that

he could since that hee sayd (though falsly) that I had whored his wife. Finding noe meanes thus to surprize mee he sent mee a letter to this Effect, that he desired to meete mee somewhere and that it might soe fall out as I might returne quietly againe. To this I replyed that if he desired to fight with mee vpon equall Termes I should vpon Assurance of the feild and faire play giue him meeting when he should any way specify the Cause And that I did not think fitt to come to him vpon any other Termes, as having bin sufficiently informed of his Plotts to Assassinate me.

After this finding hee Could take noe Aduantage against mee then in a treacherous way he resolued to assassinat mee in this manner: Hearing I was come to whitehall on horseback with two Lackeys onely he attended my coming back in a place called Scotland yard at the hither end of whitehall as you come to it from the Strand hiding him selfe here with fowre men armed with purpose to kill mee any way. I tooke horse att whitehall Gate and passing by that Place hee being Armed with a sword and dagger without giuing mee soe much as the least warning ran at mee furiously but in stead of mee wounded my horse in the Brisket, as farr as his sword could enter for the Bone; My horse herevpon starting aside he ran him again in the shoulder which though it made the horse still more Timerous yet gaue mee time to drawe my sword; His men therevpon incompassed mee and wounded my horse in three places more; This made my horse kick and fling in that manner as his men durst not come nere mee which Aduantage I tooke to strike at Sir John Aeres with all my force but hee warding the blowe both with his sword and dagger, in stead of doing him harme I broke my sword within a foote of the Hillt; Herevpon some Passangers that knew mee and obserued my horse bleeding in soe many places and soe many men together assaulting mee and my sword broken cryed to mee severall tymes, Ride away Ride away; But I scorning a base flight vpon what Termes soeuer, in stead thereof alighted the best I could from my horse. I had noe sooner put one foote vpon the Ground But Sir John Aires pursuing mee made at my horse againe which the horse perceiuing prest on mee on the side I alighted in

that manner that he threw mee downe soe that I remayned flat vpon
the Ground onely one foote hanging in the stirrop, with that piece
of a sword in my right hand; Sir John Aires herevpon ran about the
horse and was thrusting his Sword into mee when I finding my selfe
in this danger did with both my Armes reach at his Leggs, pull them
towards mee till hee fell downe backwards on his head; One of my
footemen herevpon who was a litle Shropshire boy freed my foote
out of the stirropp, The other which was a greate fellow hauing
ran away as soone as hee sawe the first assault; This gaue mee tyme
to get vpon my Leggs and to put my selfe in the best posture I could
with that poore remnant of a weapon. Sir John Aires by this time
likewise was got vp standing betwixt mee and some part of whitehall
with two men on each side of him and his brother behinde him with
at least twenty or thirty persons of his freinds or Attendants of the
Earle off Suffolke; Observing thus a body of men standing in
Oposition against mee Though to speake truly I sawe noe swords
drawne but by Sir John Aire and his men. I ran violently against Sir
John Aire But he knowing my sword had noe poynt held his sword
and dagger ouer his head as believing I would strike rather then
thrust which I had noe sooner perceiued but I put home a Thrust to
the middle of his brest that I threw him downe with soe much force,
that his head fell first to the Ground and his heeles upwards; His
men herevpon assaulted mee when one Mr. Maunsell a Glamorgan-
shire Gentleman finding soe many set against mee alone closed with
one of them, A Scotch Gentleman also Closing with another tooke
him of also, All I could well doe to those two which remayned was
to ward theire thrusts which I did with that resolution that I got
ground vpon them. Sir Iohn Aires now was gott vp a third tyme
when I making towards him with Intention to Close as thinking
that there was otherwise noe safety for mee, put by a Thrust of his
with my left hand, and soe coming within him, receiued a stab with
his dagger on my right side which ran downe my Ribbs as far as
my hipp which I feeling did with my right Elbow force his hand
together with the hillt of the dagger soe neare the vpper part of my
Right side That I made him leaue hoult; The Dagger now sticking

in mee, Sir Henry Carye afterwards Lord of Faulkland and Lord Deputy of Ireland finding the dagger thus in my Body snatcht it out; This while I being closed with Sir Iohn Aires hurt him on the head and threw him downe a third tyme, when kneeling on the Ground and bestriding him I struck at him as hard as I could with my piece of a sword and wounded him in fowre seurall places and did almost cutt of his left hand; His two men this while struck at mee but it pleased God (euen miraculously) to defend mee, for when I lifted vp my sword to strike at Sir Iohn Aires I boare of theire Blowes halfe a dozen tymes; his freinds now finding him in this danger tooke him by the head and shoulders and drew him from betwixt my Leggs, and Carrying him along with them through whitehall, at the staires whereof hee tooke boate. Sir Herbert Croft (as he told mee afterwards) mett him vpon the water vomiting all the way which I beleiue was caused by the Uiolence of the first Thrust I gaue him; his servants brother and freinds being now retyred also I remayned Master of the place and weapons, having first wrested his Dagger from him and afterwards strucken his sword out of his hand.

This being done I retyred to a freinds house in the strand, where I sent for a Surgeon who searching my wound on the right side and finding it not to bee mortall cured mee in the space of some ten dayes, during which tyme I receiued many noble Uisitts and Messages from some of the best in the Kingdome. Being now fully recouered of my hurts I desired Sir Robert Harley to goe to Sir John Airs and tell him, That though I thought he had not soe much honor left him That I could bee any way ambitious to get it, yet that I desired to see him in the feild with his sword in his hand; The answer that he sent mee was That I had whored his wife and that he would kill mee with a Musket out of a windowe; The Lords of the Privy Counsell who had first sent for my sword That they might see that litle fragment of a weapon with which I had soe behaued my selfe as perchance the like had not beene heard in any Credible way did afterwards command both him and mee to appeare before them, But I absenting my selfe on purpose sent one Humfrey Uille[1] with a Challeng to him in an Ordinary which he refusing to receiue Humfrey Uille put it vpon the poynt of his Sword and soe let it fall before him and the Company then present; The Lords of the Counsell had now taken order to apprehend Sir John Aires, when I finding nothing els was to bee done submitted my selfe likewise to them. Sir Iohn Aires had now publyshed euery where, That the Ground of his Iealousie and consequently of his Assaulting mee was drawne from the Confession of his wife the Lady Aires shee to vindicate her honor as well as to free mee from this Accusation sent a Letter to her Aunte the Lady Crooke to this purpose: That her husband Sir Iohn Aire did lye falsly in saying That I had euer whored her but most falsly of all did lye when hee said he had it from her Confession for shee had neuer said any such thing.

This letter the Lady Crooke presented to mee most oportunely as I was going to the Counsell table before the Lords, who having examined Sir John Aires concerning the Cause of his Quarrell against mee found him still persist on his wifes Confession of the Fact And now hee being withdrawne I was sent for; when the Duke of Lenox, afterwards of Richmond telling mee that was the Ground of his Quarrell and the onely excuse hee had for assaulting mee, in that manner, I desired his Lordship to peruse the Letter which I told him was giuen mee as I came into the Roome, This letter being publiquely read by a Clarke of the Counsell The Duke of Lenox then said That hee thought Sir John Aires the most miserable man living for his wife had not onely giuen him the Lye (as he found by her Letter) But his Father had disinherited him for attempting to kill mee in that barbarous fashion (which was most true as I found afterwards.) For the rest that I might Content my selfe with what I had done, It being more almost then could bee beleiued but that I had soe many wittnesses thereof, For all which reasons hee comanded mee in the name of his Majestie and theire Lordships not to send any more to Sir John Aires nor to receiue any Message from him in the way of fighting, which Commandment I obserued. Howbeit I must not omitt to tell That some yeares afterwards Sir John Aires returning from Ireland by Beaumaris where I then was, some of my servants and fellowes broke open the doores of the house where hee was and would (I beleiue) have Cutt him into pieces, but that I hearing thereof came suddainly to the house and recalled them sending him word also That I scornd to giue him that Vsage he gaue mee and that I would set him free out of the Towne, which Courtesie of mine (as I was told afterwards) he did thankfully acknowledge.

About a moneth after that Sir John Aires attempted to Assasinat mee The news thereof was carried (I know not how) to the Duke of Montmorency who presently dispatcht a Gentleman with a letter[1] to mee which I keepe and a kynde offer, That if I would come vnto him I should bee vsed as his owne sonne, neither had this Gentleman (that I know of) any other busines in England; I was told besides by this Gentleman That the duke heard I had Greater and more Enemyes then did publickly declare themselues (which indeed was true) and that he doubted I might haue a mischeife before I was aware.

My answer hereunto by Letter was That I rendered most humble thanks for his greate favour in sending to mee That noe Enemyes how greate or many soeuer could force mee out of the Kingdome, But if euer there were occasion to serue him in particular I should not faile to come, For performance whereof It hapening there was some Overtures of a Ciuill warre in France the next yeare, I sent ouer a Frensh Gentleman who attended me vnto the Duke of Montmorency expressly to tell him That if hee had occasion to vse my service in the designed warre I would bring ouer 100 horse at my owne Cost and Charges to him, which that good old Duke and Conestable tooke soe kindely That (as the Dutches of Ventedour, his Daughter told mee afterwards when I was Ambassadour) There were few days till the last of his life that hee did not speake of mee with much affection.

I can say litle more memorable concerning my selfe from the yeare 1611 when I was hurt vntill the yeare of our Lord 1614, Then that I past my Time sometimes in the Court where (I protest before God) I had more favours then I desired and sometimes in the Countrey without any memorable accident; But onely That it hapned one tyme going from St. Gillians to Abergaueny in the way to Mountgomery Castle Richard Griffiths a servant of mine being come neare a Bridge ouer Husk[1] not farr from the Towne thought fitt to water his horse But the Ryver being deepe and strong in that Place where he entred it, he was carried downe the streame; My servants that were before mee seeing this cryed allowd Dick Griffiths was Drowning, which I no sooner heard, but I put spurrs to my horse, and coming vp to the Place where I sawe him as high as the middle in water lept into the Ryver a litle below him and swimming vp to him bore him vp with one of my hands and brought him vnto the middle of the Ryver where (through Gods greate Prouidence) there was a bank of sands. Coming hither (not without some difficulty) wee rested our selues and aduised whether it were better to returne back vnto the side from whence wee came or to goe on forwards, But Dick Griffiths saying wee were sure to swimme if wee turned back and that perchance, The River might bee shallow the other way I followed his Counsell and putting my horse below him bore him vp in the manner I did formerly and swimming through the Ryver brought him safely to the other side. The horse I rid upon I remember cost mee forty pounds and was the same horse which Sir John Aires hurt vnder mee and did swimme excellently well carrying mee and his back aboue the water whereas that little nagge vpon which Richard Griffiths rid swam soe lowe that hee must needs haue drowned if I had not supported him.

I will tell one history more of this horse which I bought of my Cozen Fowler of the Grange because it is memorable. I was passing ouer a Bridg not farre from Colebrook[2] which had noe Barier on the one side and a hole in the Bridge not farre from the middle; My horse (though Lusty) yet being very Timerous and seeing besides but very litle on the right Eye started soe much at the hole That vpon a suddaine he had put halfe his body lengthwise ouer the side of the Bridge and was ready to fall into the River with his Forefoote and hinderfoote on the right side when I (forseeing the danger I was in if I fell downe) clapt my left foote together with the stirrop and spurr flat long to the left side, and soe made him leape vpon all fowre into the Ryver whence after some three or fowre plunges he brought mee to Land.

The yeare 1614 was now entring when I vnderstood that the Lowe Countrey and Spanish Army would bee in the feild that yeare; This made mee Resolue to offer my service to the Prince of Aurange who upon my coming did much wellcome mee, not suffering mee almost to eate any where but at his table and carrying mee abroad the afternoons in his Coach to partake of those entertaynments he delighted in when there was noe pressing occasion. The Low Countrey Army being now ready his Excellency prepared to goe to the feild in the way to which he tooke mee sometymes in his Coach and sometimes in a Waggon after the Lowe Countrey fashion to the greate Envy of the English and Frensh Cheife Commanders who expected that honor. Being now arrived towards Emerick, one with a most humble Petition came from a Monistary of Nunns most humbly desiring That the Souldiers might not violate theire honor nor the Monistary wherevpon I was a most humble Suitor to his Excellency to spare them which he graunted but, said hee, wee will goe and see them our selues And thus his Excellency and I and Sir Charles Morgan onely not long after going to the Monastiry found it deserted in greate part. Having put a Guard upon this Monistary his Excellency marched with his Army till wee came neare the Citty of Emericke which vpon Summoning yeilded; And now leaving a Garrison here, wee resolued to March towards Rice, This place having the Spanish Army vnder the Command of Monsieur Spinola on the one side and the Lowe Countrey Army on the other, being able to resist neither, sent word to both Armyes That which soeuer came first should haue the Place. Spinola herevpon sent word to his Excellencye That if wee intended to take Rice hee would giue him battell in a Plaine neare before the Towne. His Excellency nothing astonished hereat marched on, his Pioners making his way for the Army still through hedges and Ditches till he came to that Hedge and ditch which was next the Playne, And here drawing his men into Battell resolued to attend the Coming of Spinola into the feild; while his men were putting

Above left: *Edward Cecil; later engraving after a contemporary portrait*

Above right: *Ambrosio Spinola; engraving after a portrait by Van Dyck*

Left: *Prince Maurice of Nassau; 17th-century engraving*

in order I was soe desirous to see whether the Enemie appeared that I lept ouer a greate hedge and ditch attended onely with one Foote-man, purposing to Exchange a Pistoll Shott or two with the first I mett. I found thus some single horse in the feild, who perceiuing mee come on rid away as fast as he could as beleiuing (per chaunce) that more would follow mee, Having thus past to the further end of the feild and finding that noe Enemy shew, I returned back that I might informe his Excellency there was noe hope of fighting for anything I could perceiue. This while his Excellency having prepared all things for battell sent out five or six scouts to discouer whether the Enemy were come according to his promis; These men finding mee now coming towards them thought I was one of the Enemys which being perceiued by mee and I as litle knowing at that tyme who they were ryd up with my sword and Pistoll to encounter them and now being come within reasonable distance One of the Persons there that knew mee told his fellowes who I was wherevpon I past quietly to his Excellency and told him what I had done and that I found noe Apparance of an Army. His Excellency then caused the hedg and ditch before him to bee levelled and marcht in Front with his Army into the middle of the Feild from whence sending some of his forces to summon the Towne It yeilded without Resistance.

Our Army made that haste to come to the Place appointed for Battaile that all our Baggage and Provision were left behind, In soe much That I was without any meate but what my Footeman spared mee out of his Pockett and my Lodging that night was noe better for Extreame Raine falling at that time in the open feild I had noe shelter but was glad to get on the Top of a waggon which had straw in it and to cover my selfe with my Cloake the best I could and soe endure that stormy night. Morning being come and noe Enemy appearing I went to the Towne of Rice into which his Excellency having now put a Garrison marched on with the Rest of his Army towards Wezel before which Spinola with his Army lay And, in the way intrenching himself strongly, attended Spinolas motions. Nothing memorable hapned after this betwixt these two great Generalls for the space of many weekes.

I must not omitt yet with thankfullnes to remember a favour his Excellency did mee at this tyme for one Souldier having killed his fellow souldier in the Quarter where they were lodged which is an impardonable fault, In soe much That noe man would speake for him The poore fellow comes to mee and desires mee to begg his life of his Excellency wherevpon I demaunding whether he had euer heard of a man pardoned in this kynd, And hee saying noe I told him it was in vayne then for mee to speake; when the poor fellow writhing his neck a litle said, Sir, but were it not better you shall cast away a few words, than I loose my Life: This piece of Eloquence moved me so much that I went straight to his Excellency, and told him what the poor fellow had said, desiring him together to excuse me if upon these terms I took the boldness to speak for him: There was present at that time the Earle of Southhampton as also Sir Edward Cecill, and Sir Horace Vere, as also Monsieur de Chastillon, and divers other French Commanders; To whome his Excellency turning himself said in French, do You see this Cavalier? with all that courage you know hath yet that good nature to pray for the Life of a poor Souldier; though I had never pardon'd any before in this kind, yet I will pardon this at his request, so commanding him to be brought me, and disposed of as I thought fit, whom therefore I released and let free.

It was now so far advanced in Autumn both Armies thought of retiring themselves into their Garrisons, when a Trumpeter comes from the Spanish Army to ours with a Challenge from a Spanish Cavalier to this effect, that if any Cavalier in our Army woud fight a single combat for the sake of his Mistriss, the said Spaniard would meet him, upon assurance of the camp in our Army. This challenge being brought early in the morning was accepted by no body 'till about 10 or 11 of the clock when the report thereof coming to me, I went streight to his Excellency and told him I desired to accept the challenge; His Excellency thereupon looking earnestly upon me told me he was an old Souldier, and that he had observed two sorts of men who used to send challenges in this kind; One was of those who having lost perchance some part of their honor in the field against the Enemy, would recover it againe by a single fight. The Other was of those who sent it only to discover whether our Army had in it men effected to give trial of them selves in this kind; Howbeit if this man was a person without exception to be taken against him, he said there was none he knew, upon whome he would sooner venture the honor of his Army than my self, and this also he spoke before divers of the English and French Commanders I formerly nominated. Hereupon, by his Excellency's permission, I sent a Trumpet to the Spanish Army with this answer that if the person who would be sent were a Cavalier without reproach, I would answer him with such weapons as we should agree upon, in the place he offer'd, but my Trumpeter was scarcely arrived, as I believe, at the Spanish Army, when another Trumpeter came to ours from Spinola, saying the challenge was made without his consent, and that therefore he would not permit it; This message being brought to his Excellency with whome I then was, he said to me presently This is strange, they send a Challenge hither, and when they have done, recall it. I should be glad if I knew the true causes of it; Sir, said I, if You will give me leave, I will go to their Army, and make the like challenge, as they sent hither; It may be some scruple is made concerning the place appointed, being in your Excellency's camp, and therefore I shall offer them the combate in their own; His Excellency said, I should never have perswaded you to this course, but since you voluntarily offer it, I must not deny that which you think to be for your honor. Hereupon taking my leave of him, and desiring Sir Humphrey Tufton, a brave Gentleman to bare me company. Thus We two attended only with two Lackies rode streight towards the Spanish camp before Wezel, coming thither without any disturbance by the way. I was demanded by the Guard at the entring into their Camp, with whome I would speak, I told them with the Duke of Newbourg, whereupon a Souldier was presently sent with us to conduct us to the Duke of Newbourg's Tent, who remembring me well since he saw me at the siege of Julires, very kindly embraced me, and therewithall demanding the cause of my coming thither, I told him the effect thereof in the manner I formerly set down; to which he replied only he would acquaint the Marquis Spinola therewith, who coming shortly after to the Duke of New-bourg's Tent with a great Train of Commanders and Captains following him, he no sooner entred, but he turned to me and said, that he knew well the cause of my coming, and that the same reasons which made him forbid the Spanish Cavalier to fight a Combate in the Prince of Orange's Camp, did make him forbid it in his, and that I should be better welcome to him than I would be, and thereupon intreated me to come and dine with him; I finding nothing else to be done did kindly accept the offer, and so attended him to his Tent, where a brave dinner being put upon his Table, he placed the Duke of Newbourg uppermost at one end of the Table, and my self at the other, himself sitting below us, presenting with his own hand still the best of that meat his Carver offer'd him. He demanded of me then in Italian, Di che moriva Sigr. Francisco Vere? Of what died Sir Francis Vere? I told him, per aver niente a fare, because he had nothing to do; Spinola replied, Ed basta por un generale, and it is enough to kill a Generall and indeed that brave Commander Sir Francis Vere died not in time of War but of peace.

Taking my Leave now of the Marquis Spinola, I told him that if ever he did lead an Army against the Infidels I should adventure to be the first man that would die in that Quarrel, and together demanded Leave of him to see his Army, which he granting I took leave of him, and did at Leisure view it; Observing the difference in the Proceedings betwixt that and the Low Country Army and Fortifications as well as I could; and so returning shortly after to his Excellency related to him the success of my journey. It happened about this time that Sir Henry Wotton mediated a Peace[1] by the Kings command, who coming for that purpose to Wezel, I took occasion to go along with him into Spinola's Army, whence after a nights stay, I went on an extream rainy day through the Woods to Kysarswert[2], to the great wonder of mine host, who said all men were robbed or killed that went that way: from hence I went to Cullin, where among other things I saw the Monastary of St. Herbert;[3] from hence I went to Hydelberg, where I saw the Prince and Princess Palatine, from whome having received much good usage, I went to Ulme, and so to Augsbourg.[1] where extraordinary honor was done me, for coming into an Inn where an Ambassador from Brussels lay, the Town sent twenty great Flaggons of Wine thither, whereof they gave Eleven to the Ambassador, and nine to me, and withall some such Compliments that I found my Fame had prevented[2] my coming thither. From hence I went through Switzerland to Trent, and from thence to Venice, where I was received by the English Ambassador, Sir Dudley Carlton with much Honor; among other favors shewed mee I was brought to see a Nunne in Murano who being an Admirable beauty and together singing extreamly well, who was thought one of the Rarityes not onely of that Place but of the Tyme; we came to a Roome opposite vnto the Cloyster when she coming on the other side of the Grate betwixt vs sung soe extreamly well That when shee departed neither my Lord Ambassedor nor his Lady who were then present could finde as much as a word of fitting Language to returne her for the extraordinary Musicke shee gaue us, when being ashamed that shee should goe back without some Testemony of the sense wee had both of the Harmony of her beauty and her voyce, I sayd in Italian, *Muoia pur quando vuol non bisogna mutar ni voce ni faccia per esser un Angelo*, Dye whensoeuer you will you neither neede to Change voice nor face to bee an Angell. These words it seemed were Fatall For going thence to Rome and returning shortly afterwards I heard shee was dead in the meane tyme.

From Uenice after some stay I went to Florence where I met the Earle of Oxford and Sir Beniamin Rudier. Having seene the Rarityes of this place likewise and particularly that rare Chappell made for the house of Medici beautified on all the Inside with a Course kynde of Precious stone as also that nayle which was at the one end Iron and the other gould made soe by vertue of a Tincture into which it was putt. I went to Siena and from thence a little before the Christmas hollidays to Roome. I was noe sooner alighted at my Inne but I went straight to the English Colledge[3] where demanding for the Regent or the Master thereof a graue person not long after appeared at the doore to whome I spake in this manner, Sir I neede not tell you my Countrey when you heare my Language; I come not here to study Controuersies but to see the Antiquityes of the Place, If without scandall to the Religion in which I was borne and brought vp I may take this Liberty: I should bee glad to spend some convenient tyme here, If not, my horse is yet vnsadled and my selfe willing to goe out of Towne. The answer returned by him to mee was that he neuer heard any body before mee professe himselfe of any other Religion then what was vsed in Roome, For his part he approud much my Freedome as collecting thereby I was a person of honor, for the rest That he could giue mee noe warrant for my stay there, Howbeit that Experience did teach That those men who gaue noe affronts to the Roman Catholique Religion receiued none, wherevpon also hee demaunded my name I telling him I was called Sir Edward Herbert he replyed that he had heard men often tymes speake of mee both for learning and Courage and presently invited mee to dinner. I tould him that I tooke his Courteous offer as an Argument of his Affection That yet I desired him to excuse mee if I did not accept it The vttermost liberty I had as the tymes then were in England being already taken in coming to that Citty; Onely least they should thinke me a factious person, I thought fitt to tell him That I conceiued the Points agreed vpon on both sides were greater Bonds of Amity betwixt vs Then that the Points disagreed on could breake them, that for my part I loued euery body that was of a pious and vertuous life, and thought the Errors on what side soeuer, were more worthy Pitty then Hate. Now hauing declared my selfe thus farre I tooke my leaue of him Courteously and spent about a moneths tyme in seeing the Antiquityes of that place which first found meanes to establish soe great an Empire ouer the persons of men and afterwards ouer theire Consciences: The Articles of Confessing and Absolving sinners being a greater *Arcanum Imperii* for Gouerning the world then all the Acts invented by Statists formerly were.

After I had seene Roome sufficiently I went to Tivuly anciently called Tibur and sawe the faire Pallace and garden there as also Frascati, annciently called Tusculanum, which being done I returned to Roome and saw the Pope in Consistory. When the Pope being now ready to giue his Blessing I departed thence suddainly which gaue such suspition of mee that some were sent to apprehend mee But I going a byway escaped them and went to my Inne to take horse where I had not been now halfe an houre when the Master or Regent in the English Colledge telling me that I was accused in the Inquisition and that I could stay noe longer with any safety; I tooke this warning very kindely, Howbeit I did onely for the present chang my Lodging and soe a day or two afterwards tooke horse and went out of Roome towards Siena and from thence to Florence where after I had staid awhile I sawe Sir Robert Dudley who had the Title of Earle or Duke of Northumberland giuen him by the Emperor, and handsom Mrs. Sudel who hee carried with him out of England and was there taken for his wife. I was invited by them to a greate Feast the night before I went out of the Towne; Taking my leaue of them both I prepared for my Iourney. The next morning when I was ready to depart a Messinger came to mee and told mee That if I would accept the same Pension Sir Robert Dudley had, being two thousand Ducketts per annum, The duke would entertayne mee for his service in the Warrs against the Turks. This offer (whether procured by the meanes of Sir Robert Dudley, Mrs. Sudel or Signior Lotti my ancient friend in England) being thankfully acknowledged as a greate honor was yet refused by mee, My Intention being to serue his Excellency[1] in the Lowe Countrey war.

From hence therefore I went by Ferrara and Bologna towards Padoua, In which Vniuersity having spent some tyme to heare the learned readers there and particularly Chremonini, I left my English horses and scotch saddles there, for on them I rid all the way from the Lowe Countreys. I went by Boate to Uenice, The Lord Ambassadour Sir Dudley Carleton by this tyme had a Command to reside a while in the Court of the Duke of Savoy wherewith also his Lordshipp acquainted mee, demaunding whether I would goe thither. This offer was gladly accepted by mee both because I was desirous to see that Court and that it was in the way to the Lowe Countrey where I meant to see the warres the summer ensuing.

Coming thus in the Coach with My Lord Ambassedour to Millan, The Gouernor thereof invited My Lord Ambassedour to his house, and sometimes feasted him during his stay there, Here I heard that Famous Nunne sing to the Organ in this manner: Another Nunne beginning first to sing performed her part soe well that wee gaue her much applause for her Excellent Art and Uoyce Onely wee thought shee did sing somewhat lower then other women vsually did wherevpon also being ready to depart wee heard suddainly for wee sawe noe body That Nunne which was soe famous sing an eighth higher then the other had done; Her Uoyce was the sweetest strongest and clearest that euer I heard In the vseing whereof also she shewed that Art as ravisht vs into Admiration.

From Millan we went to Navarra[1] (as I remember) where wee were entertained by the Gouernor being a Spaniard with one of the most sumptuous feasts that euer I sawe being yet but of nine dishes in three seuerall services, The first whereof was Three Ollas podridas[2] Consisting of all choice boyld meats placed in three huge siluer Chargers which tooke vp the length of a greate Table, the meate in it being haightned vp artificially Piramidwise to a sparrow which was on the Toppe. The second service was like the former of Roste in which all manner of Fowle from the Phesant and Partridg to other Fowle lesse then them were haightned vp to a Larke, The third was in dry Sweetemeates of all sorts haightened in the like manner to a round Comfett.[3]

From thence we went to Uercelly a Towne of the duke of Savoy, frontier vnto the Spaniard with whome the duke was then in Warre, From whence passing by places of least note wee came to Turin where the Duke of Savoy his Court was. After I had refreshed my selfe here some two or three dayes, I tooke leaue of my Lord Ambassedour with Intention to goe to the Lowe Countreys and was now vpon the way thither as farre as the foote of Mount Cenis[4] when the Count Scarnafigi[5] came to me from the Duke. Ouertaking mee he brought mee a letter to this effect that the duke had heard I was a Cauellier of greate worth and desired to see the Warres, And that if I would serue him I should make my owne Condition; Finding

soe Courteous an Invitation I returned back and was Lodged by the
Duke of Savoy in a Chamber furnished with silke and gould hangings
and a very rich bed, and defraid at the dukes Charges in the English
Ambassedours house. The duke also confirmed vnto mee what the
Conte Scarnifigia had sayd and together bestowed diuers Complements on mee; I tould his highness that when I knew in what service
he pleased to imploy mee he should finde mee ready to testify the
sense I had of his princely Invitation.

It was now in the tyme of Carnevale when the Duke who loved the
Company of Ladyes and dancing as much as any Prince whosoeuer
made diuers Masks and Balls in which his owne daughters among
diuers other Ladyes danced, And here it was his manner to Place
mee always with his owne hands neare some faire Lady wishing vs
both to entertayne each other with some discourse which was a
greate Favour among the Italians; hee did many other wayes also
declare the greate esteeme he had of mee without coming yet to any
particulars The tyme of the yeare for going to the Feild being not
yet come, Onely he exercised his men often and made them ready
for his Occasions in the spring.

The duke at last resoluing how to vse my service thought fitt to
send mee to Languidoc in France to conduct 4000 men of the reformed Religion (who had promised theire Assistance in his warr)[1]
vnto Piemont. I willingly accepted his offer, soe taking my Leave of
the duke, bestowing a matter of seaventy or eighty pound among his
servants for that kinde Entertainment I had receiued. I tooke my
leaue also of my Lord Ambassedour and Sir Albertus Moreton who
was likewise imployed there and prepared for my Iourney, which for
more expedition I was desired to goe post. An old scotch Knight of
the Sandlands hearing this desired to borrow my horses as farre as
Heydelberg vpon Condition that he would vse them well by the way
and giue them good keeping in that place afterwards; The Conte
Scarnafigia was commanded to beare mee Company in this Journey
and to carry with him some Iewells which hee was to pawne at
Lions in France, and with the Money gotten for them to rayse the
Souldiers above nominated, For though the duke had put extreame

Taxations on his people in soe much That they not onely paid a certayne summe for euery horse Ox Cow or Sheepe that they kept but afterwards for euery Chimney and finally euery single person by the Pole[1] which amounted to a Pistoll, or fourteene shillings a head yet he wanted Money: At which I did not soe much wonder as at the Patience of his subiects, of whome when I demaunded how they could beare those Taxations, I haue heard some of them answer wee are not soe much offended with the duke for what he taketh from vs as thankfull to him for what he leaveth vs.

The Conte Scarnafigia and I now setting forth ryd Post all day without eating or drinking by the way, the Conte telling mee still wee should come to a good Inne at night; It was now Twilight when the Conte and I came to a solitary Inne on the Top of a Mountayne, The Hostes hearing the Noyse of our Horses came out with a Childe new borne on her left Arme and a Rush Candle in her hand; shee presently knowing the Conte de Scarnafigi tould him Ah Signior you are come in a very ill tyme, The dukes Souldiers haue beene here today and haue left mee nothing. I looked sadly vpon the Counte when he coming neare to me whispered in the Eare and said It may bee shee thinks wee will vse her as the Souldiers haue done; Goe you into the house and see whether you can finde any thing, I will goe round about the house And tis ods but I sheall meet with some hen duck or Chickens; Entring thus into the house I found for all other furniture of it the end of an Forme[2] vpon which sitting downe The Hostes came towards mee with a Rush Candle and said I protest before God that is true which I tould the Count, here is nothing to eate But you are a Gentleman me thinks it is pitty you should want; If you please I will giue you some milk out my Brests into a wooden dish I haue here. This vnexpected kindnes made that Impression in me That I remember I was neuer soe tenderly sensible of any thing, Saying God forbid I should take away thy milk from the Childe I see in thy Armes howbeit I shall take it for the greatest piece of Charity that euer I heard of, and therewithall giving her a Pistoll or a piece of gold of fourteene shillings Scarnafigi and I gott on horsebacke againe and ryd another Post and came to an Inne where though wee found very Course Faire yet hunger made vs relish it.

This Journey I remember I went over Mount Gabelet[1] by night being carryed downe that Precipice in a Cheare. A guide that went before mee bringing a Bottell of Strawe with him, and kindling pieces of it from tyme to tyme that wee might see our way: Being at the bottome of the hill I got on horseback and ryd to Burgoin[2] resoluing to rest there a while And the rather to speake truly that I had heard diuers say and particularly Sir John Finnet, and Sir Richard Newport That the hostes daughter there was the handsomest woman that euer they sawe in theire lifes; Coming to the Inne the Conte Scarnafigi wisht mee to rest there for two or three houres and he would go before to Lions to prepare busines for my Iourney to Languidoc; The Hosts daughter being not within I told her Father and Mother that I desired onely to see theire daughter as having heard her spoken of in England with soe much advantage that diuers told mee they thought her the handsomest Creature that euer they sawe; They answered that shee was gone to a Marriage and should bee presently sent for wishing mee in the meane while to take some rest vpon a bed for they sawe I needed it. Wakening now about two houres afterwards I found her sitting by mee attending when I would open mine Eyes; I shall touch a litle of her discription, her haire being of a shining Black was naturally curled in that order that a Curious woman would haue drest it, for one Curle rising by degrees aboue another and euery Bout tyed vp with a small Reband of a Nackarine[3] mixture while it was bound vp in this manner from the Poynt of her shoulder to the Crowne of her head; her Eyes which were round and black seemed to bee a Modell of her wholle beautye and in some sort of her heyre while a kynde of light or flame came from them not vnlike that which the Reband which tyed vp her haire exhibited. I doe not remember euer to haue seen a prittier Mouth or whiter teeth, breifely all her outward part seemed to become each other neither was there any thing that could bee misliked vnlesse one should say her Complexion was too browne which yet from that shadow was haightned with a good blood in her Cheekes; Her

Gowne was of a Greene Turkye Grogram cutt all into Panes of Slashes and tyed vp at the distance of about a hands breadth euery where with the same Reband with which her haire was bound, soe that her Attire seemed as Bizar as her person. I am too long in describing a Hosts daughter Howbeit I thought I might better speake of her then of diuers other beautyes held to bee the best and fairest of the tyme whom I haue often seene. In Conclusion after about an hours stay I departed thence without offering soe much as the least incivility and indeed after soe much wearines It was enough that her sight onely did refresh mee.

From hence I went straight to Lions; Entring the Gate The Guards there, after there vsuall maner demanded who I was, whence I came, and whether I went. To which while I answered I obserued one of them looked very attentiuely vpon mee and then againe vpon a paper he had in his hand; This having been done diuers tymes bred in mee a suspicion that there was noe good meaning in it and I was not deceiued in my Coniecture, For the Queene Mother[1] of France Having newly made an Edict That noe Souldiers should bee raysed in France, The Marques de RamBovillet Frensh Ambassedour at Turin sent word of my Imployment to the Marques de St. Chaumont then Gouernor of Lions as also the discription of my Person. This Edict was soe severe as they who raysed any men were to loose theire heads. In this vnfortunate Coniuncture of Affaires nothing fell out soe well as that I had not raised as yet a man; Howbeit the Guard's requiring mee to come before the Gouernor I went with him to a Church where he was at Uespers, This while I walked in the lower part of the Church, litle imagining in what danger I was in, had I leavyed any men; I had not walked there long when a single Person came to mee apparelld in a Black stuffe Suite without any Attendance vpon him, when I supposing this person to bee any man rather than the Gouernor saluted him without much Seremony, his first Question was whence I came, I answered from Turin; he demaunded then whether I would goe, I answered I was not yet resolued, His third Question was what news was at Turin, I answered That I had noe news to tell as supposing him to bee onely some busye or Inquisitive

person. The Marques herevpon called one of the Guard that Conducted mee thither and after he had whispered something in his Eare
wished mee to goe along with him which I did willingly as believing hee would bring mee to the Gouernor. This man silently leading mee out of the Church brought mee to a faire house Into which
I was noe sooner entred but he told mee I was commanded to prison
there, by him I sawe in the Church who was the Gouernor; I replyed
that I did not know him to bee Gouernor nor that this was a Prison,
and that if I were out of it againe Neither the Gouernor nor all the
Towne could bring mee into it aliue. The Master of the house
herevpon spoke mee faire And tould mee he would conduct mee to
a better chamber then any I could finde in an Inne and therevpon
brought mee to a very handsome Lodging not farre from the River;
I had not beene here halfe an houre when Sir Edward Saquevile now
Earle of Dorset hearing onely that an English man was committed
sent to know who I was and why I was inPrisond. The Gouernor
not knowing whether to lay the fault vpon my short answers to him,
or my Comission to leavy men Contrary to the Queenes Edict made
him soe doubtfull an Answer (after hee had a litle touched vpon
bothe) as dismissed him vnsatisfyed.

Sir Edward Saquevile herevpon coming to the house where I was
as soon as euer hee sawe mee imbraced mee saying Ned Herbert
what doest thou here, I answered Ned Saquevile I am glad to see
thee but I protest I know not why I am here, hee againe said Haste
thou raised any men yet for the Duke of Savoy, I replyed not soe
much as one. Then said hee I will warrant thee Though I must tell
thee the Gouernor is much offended at thy behaviour and Language
in the Church. I replyed It was impossible for mee to imagine him to
bee Gouernor that came without a guard and in such meane Clothes
as he then wore. Well, said hee I will goe to him againe and tell him
what you say and doubt not but you shalbee suddainly freed.
Herevpon returning to the Gouernor hee told him of what Family I
was and of what Condition and that I had raysed noe men and that I
knew him not to bee Gouernor, wherevpon, the Marques wisht him to
goe back that hee would come in Person to free mee out of the house.

This Message being brought mee by Sir Edward Sackvile I returned this answer onely That it was enough if hee sent order to free mee. While these Messages past a company of handsome young men and women out of I know not what Charity brought Musick vnder the Windowe and danced before mee looking often vp to see mee But Sir Edward Sacquevile being now returned with order to free mee I onely gaue them thanks out of the window and soe went along with them to the Gouernor; being come into a Greate hall where his Lady was and a Large Traine of Gentlewomen and other Persons The Gouernor with his hat in his hand demaunded of mee before all the Company whether I knew him; when his Noble Lady answering for mee said, how could hee know you when you were in the Church alone and in this habit being for the rest wholly a stranger to you? Which Ciuilitty of hers though I did not presently take notice of I did afterwards most thankfully acknowledge when I was Ambassedour in France. The Governor's next Questions were the very same he made when hee mett mee in the Church To which I made the very same answer before them all Concluding That as I did not know him hee could thinke it noe Incongruity if I answered in those Termes. The Gouernor yet was not satisfyed herewith and his noble Lady taking my part againe gaue him those reasons for my answering him in that manner That they silenced him for speaking further. The Gouernor now Turning backe I likewise after an humble Obeysance made to his Lady returned with Sir Edward Sacquevile to my Lodging. This night I passed as quietly as I could But the next morning aduised with him what I was to doe, I tould him I had receiued a greate Affront and that I intended to send him a Challenge in such Courteous Language that hee could not refuse it; Sir Edward Sacquivile by all meanes diswaded me from it, by which I perceived I was not to expect his Assistance therein, And indeed the next day he went out of Towne.

Being alone now, I thought off nothing more then how to send him a Challeng which at last I pend to this Effect: That whereas hee had giuen mee great offence without any cause I thought my selfe bound as a Gentleman to resent it and therefore desired to see him with his sword in his hand in any place hee should appoint and hoped he would nott Interpose his Authority as an excuse for not Complying with his honor on this occasion and that soe I rested his humble seruant; Finding noe body in Towne for two or three dayes, by whome I might send this Challeng I resolued for my last meanes to deliuer it in person and to obserue how hee tooke it intending to right my selfe as I could When I found he stood vpon his Authority.

This night it hapned That Monsier Tarant formerly mentioned came to the Towne; This Gentleman knowing mee well and remembring our Acquaintance both at France and Iulias wished there were some occasion for him to serue mee, I presently herevpon taking the Challeng out of my Pockett tould him he would obleig mee extreamely if hee were pleased to deliuer it And that I hoped hee might doe it with out danger since I knew the Frensh to bee soe braue a Nation That they would neuer refuse or dislike any thing that was done in an honorable and worthy way. Terant tooke the Challeng from mee and after hee had read it tould mee That the Language was civill and discreete, Nevertheles hee thought the Gouernor would not returne mee that answer I expected; howsoeuer, said he, I will deliuer it; Returning thus to my Inne and intending to sleepe quieter that night then I had done three nights before, About one of the Clock after midnight I heard a greate Noise at my doore which wakened mee, Certaine Persons knocking soe hard as if they would breake it, Besides through the Chinks thereof I sawe light; This made me presently rise in my Shirt when Drawing my sword I went to the doore and demaunded who they were? and together told them That if they came to make mee Prisoner I would rather dye with my sword in my hand, and there withall opening the Doore; I found vpon the staires some six persons armed with Halberts whome I noe sooner prepared to resist but the cheife of them told mee That they came not to mee from the Gouernor but from my good freind The Duke of Montmorency Sonne to the duke I formerly mentioned and that hee came to Towne late that night in his way from Languedoc (of which he was Gouernor) to Paris, and that hee desired mee if I loved him to rise presently and come

to him Assuring mee further That this was most true; Herevpon wishing them to retyre themselues I drest my selfe and went
with them; They conducted mee to the Greate Hall of the Gouernor
where the duke of Montmorency and diuers other Cauelliers had bin
dancing with the Ladyes, I went presently to the Duke of Montmorency who taking mee a litle aside tould mee that hee had heard
of the Passages betwixt the Gouernor and mee, And that I had sent
to him a Challeng, Howbeit that hee Conceiued that men in his
Place were not bound to answer as privat Persons for those things
they did by vertue of theire Office; Neuertheles That I should haue
satisfaction in as ample manner as I could reasonably desire;
Herevpon bringing mee with him to the Gouernor hee freely told
mee That now hee knew who I was he could doe noe lesse Then
assure mee that hee was sorry for what was done and desired mee
to take this for Satisfaction; The duke of Montmorency herevpon
said presently Ce'st assez; It is enough. I then turning to him demaunded whether he would haue taken this satisfaction in the like
Case, he said, yes. After this turning to the Gouernor, I demaunded
the same Question to which he answered That he would haue taken
the same satisfaction and a lesse too, wherevpon I kissing my hand
gaue it him who embraced mee and soe this business ended. Wherevpon after some Complements past betweene the Duke of Montmorency and my selfe who remembred the greate love his father
bore mee which he desired to Continue in his person, and putting
mee in mynde also of our being educated together for a while
demaunded whether I would goe with him to Paris; I tould him
That I was engaged to goe to the Lowe Countreys, But that wheresoeuer I was I should bee his most humble servant.

My Imployment with the Duke of Savoy in Languidoc being thus
ended I went from Lions to Geneva where I found also my Fame had
prevented my Cominge For the next morning after my Arriuall
The state taking notice of mee sent a Messinger in theire Name to
Congratulat my being there and presented mee with some Flaggons
of Wyne desiring mee (if I staid there any while) to see theire
Fortifications and give my opinion of them which I did and tould

them I thought they were weakest where they thought themselues strongest which was on the hilly part where indeed they had made greate Fortifications; yet as it is a Rule in Warre That whatsoeuer may bee made by Art may bee destroyd by Art againe I conceiued they had neede to feare the Approach of an Enemy on that part rather then any other. They replyed That diuers greate Souldiers had tould them the same, and that they would giue the best order they could to serue themselues on that side.

Having rested here some while to take Physick (my health being a litle broken with long Trauell) I departed after some fortnights stay to Basil where taking boate vpon the Ryver I came at length to Stratsbourg, and from thence went to Heydelbourg, where I was receiv'd again by the Prince Elector[1] and Princess with much kindness, and viewed at leisure the fair Library there, the Gardens and other Rarities of the Place, and here I found my Horses I lent to St. Islands[2] in good plight, which I then bestowed upon some Servants of the Prince in way of Retribution for my Welcome thither. From hence Sir George Calvert and my self went by Water for the most part to the Low Countrys where taking Leave of each other, I went straight to his Excellency who did extraordinarily welcome me, insomuch that it was observ'd that he did never outwardly make so much of any one as my self.

It hapned this summer that the Low Countrey Army was not drawn into the Field, so that the Prince of Orange past his Time in playing at Chess with me after dinner, or in going to Reswick[3] with him to see his great Horses or in making Love; In which also He used me as his Companion, yet so that I saw nothing openly more than might argue a civil Familiarity. When I was at any time from him I did by his good leave endeavour to raise a Troop of Horse for the Duke of Savoy's service, as having obtained a Commission to that purpose for My Brother William then an Officer in the Low Country: having these Men in readiness I sent word to the Count Scarnafigi thereof who was now Embassador in England, telling him that if he would send money My Brother was ready to go. Scarnafigi answered me that he expected money in England, and that as soon as he receiv'd it, he would send over so much as would pay an hundred horse, but a Peace betwixt him and the Spaniard being concluded not long after at Asti,[1] the whole charge of keeping this Horse fell upon me, without ever to this day receiving any recompence.

Winter now approaching and nothing more to be done for that year, I went to the Brill[2] to take shipping for England, Sir Edward Conway who was then Governor at that Place, and afterwards Secretary of State, taking notice of my being there came to me, and invited me every day to him, while I attended only for a Wind; which serving at last for my journey, Sir Edward Conway conducted me to the Ship, into which as soon as I was entred he caused six Pieces of Ordnance to be discharged for my Farewell, I was scarce gone a League into the Sea, when the Wind turned contrary and forced me back again: Returning thus to the Brill Sir Edward Conway welcomed me as before, and now after some three or four days, the wind serving he conducted me againe to the Ship and bestowed six Valleys of Ordnance upon me; I was now about half way to England, when a most cruel Storm arose which tore our Sails and spent our Mast, insomuch that the Master of our Ship gave us all for lost, as the wind was extream high and together contrary, we were carried at last though with much difficulty back again to the Brill, where Sir Edward Conway did congratulate my escape, saying he believed certainly that (considering the weather) I must needs be cast away.

After some stay here with my former welcome the wind being now fair, I was conducted again to my ship by Sir Edward Conway, and the same Volleys of Shot given me, and was now scarce out of the haven when the wind again turned contrary, and drove me back; This made me resolve to try my fortune here no longer; hiring a smal Barque therefore I went to the Sluice and from thence to Ostend, where finding Company, I went to Brussells. In the Inn where I lay here an Ordinary was kept, to which divers Noblemen and Principall Officers of the Spanish Army resorted; Sitting among These at Dinner the next day after my arrival, no man knowing me or informing himself who I was, They fell into discourse of divers matters in Italian, Spanish, and French, and at last Three of them One after another began to speak of King Iames my Master in a very scornfull manner; I thought with my self that then if I was a base Fellow, I need not take any Notice thereof, since no man knew me to be an English Man, or that I did so much as understand their Language; But my heart burning within me, I putting of my Hat arose from the Table, and turning my self to those that sat at the upper end who had said nothing to the King my Master's prejudice, I told them in Italian, Son Inglese, I am an English Man, and should be unworthy to live if I suffer'd these words to be spoken of the King my Master, and therewithall turning my self to those who had injured the King, I said You have spoken falsely, and I will fight with you all; Those at the upper end of the Table finding I had so much reason on my part did sharply check those I questioned, and to be brief made them ask the Kings forgiveness, wherewith also the Kings health being drank round about the Table, I departed thence to Dunkirk and thence to Graveling,[1] where I saw though unknown, an English Gentlewoman enter into a Nunnery there; I went thence to Callice, it was now extream foul weather, and I could find no Master of a Ship willing to adventure to Sea; howbeit my impatience was such, that I demanded of a poor fisherman there whether he would go, he answered that his Ship was worse than any in the Haven as being open above and without any Deck, besides that it was old, but saith he, I care for my life as litle as You do, and if you will go, my boat is at your service.

I was now scarce out of the Haven when a high grown Sea had almost overwhelmed us, the waves coming in very fast into our Ship, which we laded out again the best we could; Notwithstanding which we expected every minute to be cast away. It pleased God yet before we were gone six Leagues into the Sea to cease the Tempest and give us a fair passage over to the Downs, where after giving God thanks for my delivery from this the most needless danger that ever I did run, I went to London. I had not been here ten days when a Quartuan Ague seised on me which held me for a

year and an half without intermission, and a year and an half longer
at Spring and fall, the good days I had during all this sickness I imployed in Study, the ill being spent in as sharp and long fitts as I
think ever any man endured, which brought me at last to be so lean
and yellow that scarce any man did know me; It hapned during this
sickness, that I walked abroad one day towards White-Hall, where
meeting one Emerson who spoke very disgracefull words of Sir
Robert Harley being then my dear Friend, my weakness could not
hinder me to be sensible of my Friend's dishonor, shaking him therefore by a long beard he wore, I stept a litle aside and drew my sword
in the Street, Captain Thomas Scriven a friend of mine being not
far of on one side, and divers friends of his on the other side; All that
saw me wondred how I could go, being so weak and consumed as I
was, but much more that I would offer to fight, howsoever Emerson
instead of drawing his sword, ran his way into Suffolk House, and
afterwards informed the Lords of the Counsell of what I had done,
Who not long after sending for me, did not so much reprehend my
taking part with my Friend as that I would adventure to fight being
in such a bad condition of health; Before I came wholy out of my
Sickness, Sir George Uillers afterwards Duke of Buckingham came
into the King's favor, This Cavalier meeting me accidentally at the
Lady Stanops house came to me and told me he had heard so much
of my worth, as he would think himself happy if by his credit with
the King, he could do me any Service. I humbly thankt him But
told him that for the present I had need of nothing so much as of
health, but that if ever I had ambition, I should take the boldness to
make my Address by him.

I was no sooner perfectly recover'd of this long Sickness, but the
Earle of Oxford and my Self resolved to raise two Regiments for the
service of the Venetians; while we were making ready for this
Iourney, the King having an occasion to send an Ambassador into
France required Sir George Uillers to present him with the Names
of the fittest Men for that imployment that he knew, whereupon
eighteen names among which Mine was being written in a paper
were presented to him. The King presently chose me, yet so as he

desired first to have the approbation of his Privy Counsel who confirming his Majesties choice sent a Messenger to my house among
Gardens near the old Exchange,[1] requiring me, to come presently to
them, My self litle knowing then the Honor intended me, askt the
Messenger whether I had done any fault that the Lords sent for
me so suddainly, wishing him to tell the Lords that I was going to
Dinner and would afterwards attend them. I had scarce dined when
another Messenger was sent, this made me hasten to Whitehall where
I was no sooner come, but the Lords saluted me by the Name of Lord
Ambassador of France. I told their Lordships thereupon that I was
glad it was no worse, and that I doubted that by their speedy sending
for me, some Complaint, though false might have been made against
me.

My first Commission was to renew the Oath of Alliance[2] betwixt
the Two Crowns, for which purpose I was extraordinary Ambassador
which being done, I was to reside there as ordinary; I had receiv'd
now about six or seven hundred pounds towards the charges of my
Iourney, and lockt it in certaine Coffers in my house, when the night
following about one of the clock I could hear divers men speak and
knock at the Door, in that part of the house where none did lie but
my Self, my Wife, and her Attendants, my Servants being lodged in
an other house not far of; as soon as I heard the Noise I suspected
presently they came to rob me of my Money, howsoever I thought
fit to rise and go to the Window to know who they were. The first
word I heard was, darest Thou come down Welch Man, which I
no sooner heard but taking a sword in one hand and a litle Target
in the other, I did in my shirt run down the stairs, open the doors
suddenly, and charged 10 or 12 of them with that Fury, that they
ran away, some throwing away their Halberts, others hurting their
fellows to make them go faster in a narrow way they were to pass;
In which disorder'd manner I drove them to the middle of the street
by the Exchange, where finding my bare feet hurt by the Stones I
trod on, I thought fit to return home, and leave them to their
flight. My Servants hearing the noise by this time were got up, and
demanded whether I would have them pursue those Rogues that

fled away, but I answering that I thought they were out of Reach, We returned home together.

While I was preparing my self for my journey it happened that I passing through the Inner Temple one day And encountering Sir Robert Uaughan[1] in this Countrey, some harsh words past betwixt us which occasioned him, at the perswasion of others whom I will not nominate, to send me a Challenge; This was brought me at my House in Black-fryars by Captain Charles Price upon a Sunday about one of the Clock in the afternoon, when I had read it, I told Charles Price that I did ordinarily bestow this day in Devotion, Nevertheless that I would meet Sir Robert Vaughan presently, and gave him thereupon the length of my sword demanding whether he brought any Second with him, to which Charles Price replying that he would be in the field with him, I told my Brother Sir Henry Herbert then present thereof who readily offering himself to be my Second, nothing was wanting now but the Place to be agreed upon betwixt us, which was not far from the waterside near Chelsey. My Brother and I taking boat presently, came to the Place, where after We had stayd about two hours in vain, I desired my Brother to go to Sir Robert Uaughan's Lodging, and to tell him that I now attended his coming a great while, and that I desired him to come away speedily; hereupon my Brother went and after a while returning back again, he told me they were not ready yet; I attended then about an hour and an half longer, but as he did not come yet, I sent my Brother a second time to call him away, and to tell him I catcht cold, nevertheless that I would stay there 'till sun set. My Brother yet could not bring him along, but returned himself to the Place where We stay'd together till half an hour After Sunset and then returned home.

The next day the Earle of Worcester, by the King's Command, forbid me to receive any Message or Letter from Sir Robert Uaughan, and advertised me withall that the King had given him charge to end the business betwixt us, for which purpose he desired me to come before him the next day about two of the Clock, at which time after the Earle had told me, that being now made Ambassador and a publick Person, I ought not to entertain private Quarrels, after which without much adoe, he ended the business betwixt Sir Robert Vaughan and my Self; It was thought by some that this would make me loose my Place, I being under so great an obligation to the King for my Imployment in France, but Sir George Uillers afterwards Duke of Buckingham told me he would warrant me for this one time, but I must do so no more:

I was now almost ready for my Iorney, and had received already as choice a Company of Gentlemen for my Attendants as I think ever followed Ambassador, when some of my Private Friends told me that I was not to trust so much to my pay from the Exchequer, but that it was necessary for me to take Letters of Credit with me for as much money as I could well procure: Informing my Self hereupon who had furnished the last Ambassador, I was told of one Monsier Savage a French man; coming to his house I demanded whether he would help me with moneys in France, as he had done to the last Ambassador; he said, he did not know me, but would inform himself better who I was; departing thus from him I went to Sigr. Burlamacchi a man of great credit in those times, and demanded of him the same, His answer was that he knew me to be a man of honor, and I had kept my word with every body, whereupon also going to his Study gave me a Letter of Credit to One Monsieur de Langherac in Paris for 2000 l. Sterling, I then demanded what Security he expected for this money; he said, he would have nothing but my promise, I told him he had put a great obligation upon me and that I would strive to acquit my Self of it the best I could.

Having now a good Sum of Money in my Coffers and this Letter of Credit, I made ready for my Iourney; The day I went out of London I remember was the same in which Queen Ann was carried to Burial,[1] which was a sad spectacle to all that had occasion to honor Her. My first nights journey was to Gravesend, where being at Supper in my Inn, Monsieur Savage formerly mentioned came to me and told me that whereas I had spoken to him for a Letter of Credit, he had made one which he thought would be to my contentment. I demanded to whom it was directed, he said to Monsieur Tallemant and Rambouillet[2] in Paris; I asked then what they were worth, he said above one hundred thousand Pounds sterling, I demanded for how much this Letter of Credit was, he said for as much as I should have need of; I asked what security he required, he said nothing but My word which he had heard was inviolable.

From Gravesend, by easy journeys I went to Dover where I took shipping with a Train of an hundred and odd persons, and arrived shortly after at Calice, where I remember my Cheer was twice as good as at Dover, and my reckoning half as cheap, from whence I went to Boulogne Monstrevile, Abbevile, Amiens, and in two days thence to St. Dennis near Paris, where I was met with a great Train of Coaches that were sent to receive me, as also by the Master of the Ceremonies, and Monsieur Memmon[1] my fellow Scholar, with Monsieur Disancour, who then kept an Academy, and brought with him a brave Company of Gentlemen on great Horses to attend me into Town.

It was now somewhat late when I entred into Paris upon a Saturday night; I was but newly setled in my Lodging when a Secretary of the Spanish Ambassador there told me that his Lord desired to have the first Audience from me, and therefore requested he might see me the next morning, I replyed that it was a day I gave wholy to Devotion, and therefore intreated him to stay 'till some more convenient time; The Secretary replyed that his Master did hold it no less holy, howbeit that his respect to me was such that he would prefer the desire he had to serve me before all other considerations; howsoever I put him off 'till Monday following.

Not long after I took a House in Fauxbourgs St Germains Rue Tournon, which cost me 200 l. sterling yearly; having furnisht the house richly, and lodged all my Train, I prepared for a Iourney to Tours and Touraine where the French Court then was. Being come hither in extream hot weather I demanded Audience of the King and Queen, which being granted I did assure the King of the great Affection the King my Master bore him, not only out of the Ancient Alliance betwixt the two Crowns, but because Henry the Fourth and the King my Master had stipulated with each Other, that whensoever any one of them died, the Survivor should take care of the others

Child: I assured him further that no charge was so much imposed upon me by my Instructions as that I should do good offices betwixt both Kingdoms, and therefore that it were a great fault in me, if I behaved my Self otherwise than with all respect to his Majesty; This being done I presented to the King a Letter of Credence from the King my Master: The King assured me of a Reciprocall Affection to the King my Master, and of my particular Welcome to his Court; His words were never many as being so extream a Stutterer, that he would sometimes hold his Tongue out of his Mouth a good while before he could speak so much as one word. He had besides a double Row of Teeth, and was observed seldom or never to spit or blow his Nose, or to sweat much though he were very laborious and almost indefatigable in his exercises of Hunting and Hawking to which He was much addicted. Neither did it hinder him though he was burst in his body, as we call it, or Herniosus, for he was noted in those his sports though often times on foot to tire not only his Courtiers but even his Lackies; being equally insensible as was thought either of heat or cold; His Understanding and natural parts were as good as could be expected in one that was brought up in so much ignorance, which was on purpose so done that he might be the longer governed; howbeit he acquired in time a great knowledge in Affairs as conversing for the most part with wise and active Persons. He was noted to have two Qualities incident to all who were ignorantly brought up, Suspicion and Dissimulation: For as ignorant Persons walk so much in the Dark, they cannot be exempt from fear of Stumbling, and as they are likewise deprived of or deficient in those true Principles by which they should govern both Publick and Private actions in a wise, solid, and demonstrative way, they strive commonly to supply these imperfections with covert Arts, which though it may be sometimes excusable in necessituous Persons, and be indeed frequent among those who negotiate in smal matters, yet condemnable in Princes, who proceeding upon foundations of Reason and strength ought not to submit themselves to such poor helps; Howbeit I must observe that neither his fears did take away his courage, when there was occasion to use it, nor his dissimulation extend itself to the doing of private mischiefs to his Subjects either of the one or the other Religion. His favorite was one Monsieur De Luynes, who in his Nonage gained much upon the King by making Hawkes fly at all Litle Birds in his Gardens, and by making some of those Litle Birds againe catch Butter Flies. And had the King used him for no other purpose, he might have been tolerated; but as, when the King came to a Riper Age, the Government of Publick affairs was drawn cheifly from his Counsells, not a few Errors were committed. The Queen Mother, Princes, and Nobles of that Kingdome repining that his advices to the King should be so prevalent, which also at last caused a civil War[1] in that Kingdome. How unfit this man was for the Credit he had with the King may be argued by this, That when there was Question made about some business in Bohemia, he demanded whether it were an Inland Country or lay upon the Sea: And thus much for the pressent of the King and his Favorite.

After my Audience with the King, I had another from the Queen being Sister to the King of Spain, I had litle to say unto her, but some Complements on the King my Master's Part, but such complements as her Sex and Quality were capable of: This Queen was exceeding fair, like those of the House of Austria, and together of so mild and good a Condition, she was never noted to have done ill Offices to any, but to have mediated as much as was possible for her in satisfaction of those who had any Suit to the King, as far as their cause would bear. She had now been married divers years without having any Children, though so ripe for them that nothing seemed to be wanting on her part. I remember her the more particularly that She shewed publickly at my Audiences that favor to me as not only my Servants but divers others took notice of it: After first Audience I went to see Monsieur de Luynes and the Principall Ministers of State, as also the Princes and Princesses and Ladies then in the Court, and particularly the Princess of Conti, from whom I carried the Scarf formerly mentioned. And this is as much as I shall declare in this place concerning my Negotiation with the King and State; my purpose being, if God sends me Life, to set them forth a part as having the Copies of all my dispatches in a great Trunk in my house at London,[1] and considering that in the time of my stay there, there were divers Civil Wars in that Country, and that the Prince, now King, passed with my Lord of Buckingham and others through France into Spain. And the Business of the Elector Palatine in Bohemia and the Battle of Prague,[2] and divers other memorable accidents both of State and War happened during the time of my Imployment; I conceive a Narration of them may be worth the seeing to them who have it not from a better hand, I shall only therefore relate here as they come into my memory, certain litle passages which may serve in some part to declare the History of my Life.

Coming back from Tours to Paris I gave the best order I could concerning the expences of my House, Family and Stable, that I might setle all things as near as was possible in a certaine Course, allowing according to the manner of France so many pounds of Beef, Mutton, Ueal, and Pork, and so much also in Turkeys, Capons, Phcasants, Partridges, and all other Fowles, as also Pyes and Tarts after the French manner, and after all this a dozen dishes of sweetmeats every meal constantly: The ordering of these things was the heavier to mc, that my Wife flatly refused to come over into France, as being now entred into a dropsie, which also had kept her without Children for many years. I was constrained therefore to make use of a Steward who was understanding and diligent but no very honest man: My chief Secretary was William Boswell, now the King's Agent in the Low-Countrys: My Secretary for the French Tongue was one Monsieur Ozier who afterwards was the Kings Agent in France. The Gentleman of my Horse was Monsieur de Meny, who afterwards commanded 1000 Horse in the Wars of Germany and proved a very gallant Gentleman. Mr. Crofts[3] was one of my Principal Gentlemen and afterwards made the Kings Cupbearer, and Thomas Carew that excellent Wit, the Kings Carver. Edmund Taverner whom I made my under-Secretary, was afterwards cheif Secretary to the Lord Chamberlaine, and one Mr. Smith Secretary to the Earl of Northumberland; I nominate these, and could many more that came to very good Fortunes afterwards,

because I may verifie that which I said before concerning the Gentlemen that attended me.

When I came to Paris the English and French were in very ill intelligence with each other, insomuch that one Buckly coming then
to me said he was assaulted and hurt upon Pontneuf only because
he was an English Man. Nevertheless after I had been in Paris about
a Month, All the English were so wellcome thither, that no other
Nation was so acceptable amongst them, insomuch that my Gentlemen having a Quarrel with some debauched French who in their
drunkenness Quarrelled with them, Divers principall Gentlemen of
that Nation offered themselves to assist my People with their Swords.

It happened one day that my Cozen Oliver Herbert[1] and George
Radny being Gentlemen who attended me, and Henry Whittingham
my Butler had a Quarrell with some French upon I know not what
frivolous occasion. It happened My Cozen Oliver Herbert had for
his Opposite a Fencer belonging to the Prince of Condy, who was
dangerously hurt by him in divers Places; but as the house or hostel
of the Prince of Condy was not far of and himself well beloved in
those Quarters, the French in great multitudes arising, drove away
the three above mentioned into my hous pursueing them within
the Gates; I perceiving this at a Window ran out with my sword,
which the People no sooner saw but they fled again as fast as ever
they entred; howsoever the Prince of Condy his Fencer was in that
danger of his Life, that Oliver Herbert was forced to fly france,
which that he might do the better, I paid the said Fencer 200 Crowns
or 60 pounds Sterling for his hurt and Cures.

The Plague being now hot in Paris, I desired the Duke of Montmorency to lend me the Castle of Merlon where I lived in the time
of his most Noble Father, which he willingly granted. Removing
thither I injoyed that sweet Place and Countrey wherein I found not
a few that welcomed me out of their ancient Acquaintance. On the
one side of me was the Baron de Montaterre of the reformed Religion, and Monsieur de Boute Ville on the other, who though Young
at that time proved afterwards to be that brave Cavelier which all
France did so much celebrate. In both their Castles Likewise were

Ladies of much Beauty and discretion and particularly a Sister of Bouteville thought to be one of the Cheif Perfections of the Time, whose Company yielded some divertisement when my Publick Occasions did suffer it.

Winter being now come I returned to my house in Paris, and prepared for renewing the Oath of Alliance betweene the two Crownes For which as I said formerly I had an extraordinary Commission Netherheles the King put of the Busines to as long a tyme as he well could. In the meane while Prince Henry of Nasso brother to Prince Maurice coming to Paris was met and much wellcomed by mee as being obliged to him noe lesse than to his brother in the Lowe Countreys. This Prince and all his Traine was feasted by mee at Paris with 100 dishes costing as I remember in all 100 £.

The French King at last resolving vpon a day for performing the Seremony betwixt the Two Crownes abouementioned My Selfe and all my Traine put our selues into that sumptuous Equipage That I remember it Cost mee one way or another aboue a thousand pound. And truly the magnificence of it was such as a litle Frensh booke[1] was presently printed thereof. This being done I resided here in the Quality of an Ordinary Ambassedour.

And now I shall mention some particular Passages concerning my selfe without entring yet any way into the wholle frame and Context off my Negotiation reserving it (as I said before) to a particular Treatise; I spent my Time much in the visitts of the Princese, Counsell of State and greate Persons of the Frensh Kingdome, who did euer punctually requite my Uisitts, The like I did also to the Cheife Ambassedours there, Among whome The Uenetian, Lowe Countrey, Savoy, and the vnited Princes in Jermany Ambassedors did beare mee that Respect That they vsually mett in my house to aduise together concerning the great Affaires of that Tyme, For as the Spaniard then was soe potent That he seemed to affect an vniuersal Monarchy All the Abouementioned Ambassedors did in one Comon Interest strive to oppose him; All our Endeavors yet could not hinder but that hee both publiquely prevayled in his Attempts abroad, and priuately did Corrupt diuers of the principall Ministers of state in this

Kingdome. I came to discouer this by many wayes but by none more effectually then by the meanes of an Italian who returned ouer by letters of Exchang the Moneys the Spanish Ambassedour receiued for his Occasions in France; For I perceiued That when the said Italian was to receiue any extraordinary greate summe of money for the Spanish Ambassedors vse the wholle face of Affaires was presently Changed In soe much that neither my reason nor the Ambassedors abouementioned (how valid soeuer) could prevayle, Though yet afterwards wee found means together to reduce Affaires to theire former Traine vntill some other new greate Summe coming to the Spanish Ambassedors hands and from thence to the aforesaid Ministers of state, altered all. Howbeit diuers visitts past betweene the Spanish Ambassedor and my selfe; In one of which he tould mee that though our Interests were diuers yet wee might Continue Freindship in our particular persons, For said hee It can bee noe occasion of Offence betwixt vs That Each of vs striue the best hee can to serue the King his Master. I disliked not his Reason Though yet I could not omitt to tell him That I would maintaine the dignity of the King my Master the best I could And this I said because The Spanish Ambassedour had taken place of the English in the Tyme of Henry 4 in this fashion; They both meeting in an Anty Chamber to the Secretary of State the Spanish Ambassedor leaning to the wall in that posture that hee tooke the hand of the English Ambasse-dor said publiquely I hould this place in Right of the King my Master; which small Puntilio being not resented by our Ambassedor at that tyme, gaue the Spaniard occasion to Bragg that hee had taken the hand from our Ambassedour. This made mee more watchfull to regaine the honor which the Spaniard pretended to haue gotten herein, soe that although the Ambassedour in his Uisitts often re-peated the words abouementioned being in Spanish, *Que cada vno haga lo que pudiere por su amo*: Let euery man do the best he can for his Master, I attended the occasion to right my Master. It hapned one day that both of vs going to the Frensh King for our seuerall Affaires The Spanish Ambassedor between Paris and Estampas being vpon his way before mee in his Coach with a Traine of about 16 or 18 persons on horsebacke, I following him in my Coache with about ten or twelue horse found that either I must goe the Spanish Pace which is slowe or if I hasted to passe him That I must hazzard the suffering of some Affront like vnto that our former Ambassedor receiued. Proposing herevpon to my Gentlemen the wholle Busines I tould them that I meant to redeeme the honor of the King my Master some way or other demaunding further whether they would assist mee, which they promising I byd the Coachman driue on; The Spanish Ambassador seeing mee approach who imagined what my Intention was sent a Gentleman to mee to tell mee hee desired to salute mee, which I accepting The Gentleman returned to the Ambassedor who allighting from his Coach attended mee in the middle of the highway; which being perceiued by mee I alighted also when some extrauegant Complements having past betwixt vs The Spanish Ambassedor tooke his leave of mee and went to a dry ditch not farre of vpon pretence of making water but indeed to hould the vpper hand of mee while I past by in my Coach which being obserued by mee I left my Coach and getting vpon a spare horse I had there ryd into the said dry ditch and telling him allowd that I knew well why hee stood there byd him afterward get to his Coache for I must ride that way. The Spanish Ambassedour who vnderstood mee well went away herevpon to his Coach grumbling and discontented though yet neither hee nor his Traine did any more but looke one vpon another in a Confused manner; My Coach this while passing by the Ambassedour on the same side I was, I shortly after left my Horse and gott into it. It hapned this while That one of my Coach horses having lost shooe I thought fitt to stay at a Smiths Fordg, about a quarter of a myle before; This shooe yet could not bee put on soe soone but that the Spanish Ambassedor overtooke and might indeede haue past vs but that he thought I would doe him another Affront; Attending therefore the Smiths leasure he stayd in the high waye to our noe litle Admiration vntill my horse was shod. We continued our Iourney to Estampas: The Spanish Ambassedour following vs still at a good distance.

I should scarce haue mentioned this Passage but that the Spaniards stand soe much vpon theire Pundonores,[1] For confirming whereof I haue thought fitt to remember the answer a Spanish Ambassedor made to Philip the Second of Spaine who finding fault with him for neglecting a busines of greate Importance in Italy because hee could not agree with the Frensh Ambassedor about some such Pundonore as this, said to him, *Como a dexado vno cosa di importancia por vna Ceremonia*; How? have you lost a busines of Importance for a Seremonye. The Ambassedor bouldly replyed to his Master, *Como por vna Ceremonia? Vuessa magestad misma no es sino vna Ceremonia.* How for a Seremony? Your Majesties selfe are but a Seremony. Howsoeuer the Spanish Ambassedor taking noe Notice publiquely of the Advantage I had of him herein dissembled it as I heard till hee could finde some fitt Occasion to resent this Passage which yet hee neuer did to this Day.

Among the Uisitts I rendred to the Grandes of France One of the principall I made was to that braue Generall the Duke of Lesdivuigeres who was now growne very old and Deafe; His first words to mee were Monsieur you must doe mee the honor to speake high for I am deafe: My Answer to him was, Soe were you borne to Command and not to obey. It is enough if others haue Eares to heare you. This Complement tooke him much, And indeed I haue a Manuscript[2] of his military Precepts and Obseruations which I value very greatly.

I shall relate now some things Concerning my selfe which though they may seeme scarce Credible yet I protest before God are true; I had beene now in France about a yeare and a halfe when my Taylor Andre Uonly[3] of Basil (who now lives in black Fryers) demaunded of mee halfe a yard of Satin to make mee a Suite more then I was accustomed to giue, Of which when I required a reason saying, I was not fatter now then when I came to France, he answered It was true but you are taller, wherevnto when I would giue noe Credit he brought his old measures and made it appeare That they did not reach to theire just places; I tould him I knew not how this hapned but howsoeuer he should haue halfe yard more and that when I came into England I would cleare the Doubt, for a litle before my

The Château of Vincennes; 17th-century engraving by Poilly and Perelle

Charles d'Albert, Duc de Luynes; 17th-century engraving

George Villiers, Duke of Buckingham; drawing by Rubens

departure thence I remember That William Earle of Penbrooke and my selfe did measure haights together at the request of the Countesse of Bedford and hee was then higher then I by about the Breadth of my litle finger: At my returne therefore into England I measured againe with the same Earle and to both our greate wonders found my selfe taller then hee by the Breadth of a litle Finger: which growth of myne I could attribute to noe other cause but to my Quartine Ague formerly mentioned, which when it quitted mee left mee in a more perfect health then I formerly enioyed, and indeede disposed mee to some follyes which I afterwards repented and doe still repent of. But as my wife refused to come over and my Temptations were greate I hope the faults I committed are the more pardonable; Howsoeuer I can say truly that whether in France or England I was never in Bawdyhouse nor vsed my pleasures intemperatly and much lesse did accompany them with that dissimulation and falshood which is comonly found in men addicted to love women: To conclude this Passage which I vnwillingly mention I must protest againe before God that I neuer delighted in that or any other sinne and that if I transgressed sometimes in this Kynde It was to avoyd a greater ill, as abhorring any thing that was against Nature For certainly If I had been prouided with a lawfull remedy I should haue fallen into noe Extrauagancy: I could extenuate my fault by telling Circumstances which would haue operated I doubt vpon the Chastest of mankind, but I forbeare; these things being not fitt to be spoken of for though the Philosophers haue accounted this Act to be *inter honesta factu*: where neither Iniury nor Uiolence was offered, yet they euer reckoned it among the *Turpia dictu*; I shall therefore onely tell some things alike strange of my selfe.

I waighed my selfe in Ballances often with men lower than my selfe by the head, and in theire bodyes slenderer, and yet was found lighter then they, as Sir John Dauers Knight[1] and Richard Griffiths now living can witnes with both whome I haue been waighed, I had also and haue still a pulse on the Crowne of my head; It is well knowne to those that wayt in my Chamber That the shirts waste Coates and other Garments I weare next my body are sweete beyond what either easily can bee beleiued or hath bin obserued in any els which sweetenes also was found to bee in my Breath aboue others before I vsed to take Tobacco which towards my later tyme I was forced to take against Certaine Rhumes and Catarres that trouble mee which yet did not taint my Breath for any long tyme. I scarce euer felt could in my life though yet soe subiect to Cattars that I think noe man euer was more Obnoxious to it, All which I doe in a familiar way mention to my Posterity though otherwise they may bee thought scarce worth the writing.

The Effect of my sending into France by the King my master being to hold all good Intelligence betwixt both Crownes my Imployment was both noble and pleasing and my paynes not great France having noe designe at that Tyme vpon England And King James being that pacifike Prince all the world knew. And thus besides the Times I spent in Treaties and Negotiations I had either with the Ministers of State in France, or Forraigne Ambassedors residing in Paris, I had spare tyme not onely for my Booke but for Visits to diuers Grandes for litle more ends then obtayning some Intelligence of the Affaires of that Kingdome and Ciuill Conuersation To which theire free, generous and cheerefull Company was noe litle motive, Persons of all Quality being soe addicted to haue mutuall Entertaynment of each other, That in Calme weather one might finde all the noble and good Company in Paris of both sexes either in the Garden of the Tuilleries or in the Parke of Bois de Vicennes they thinking it almost an Inciuillity to refuse theire presence and free discourse to any who were Capable of coming to those places either vnder the recommendation of good Parts or but soe much as handsome clothes and a good Equipage; when fowle weather was they spent theire tyme in Uisits at each others houses where they interchanged ciuill Discourses or heard Musick or fell a dancing vsing according to the manner of that Countrey all the reasonable Libertyes they could with theire Honor; while theire manner was either in the garden of the Twilleryes or elsewhere If any one discoursing with a Lady did see some other of good fashion approach to her he would leave her and goe to some other Lady, he who conuersed with her at that time quitting her also and going to some other: That soe Addresses might be made equall and free to all without scruple on any part Neither was exception made or Quarrell begun vpon these Termes.

It hapned one day that being ready to returne from the Tuilleryes about eight of the clock in the Summer, with Intention to write a dispatch to the King about some Intelligence I had receiued there, That the Queene attended with some principall Ladyes (without soe much as one Cauellier) did enter the Garden. I staid on the one side of an Alley there to doe my Reuerence to her and the rest and soe to returne to my house when the Queene[1] perceiuing mee staid a while as if shee expected I should attend her, But as I stirrd not more then to giue her that greate Respect I owed her The Princesse of Conte who was next called mee to her and said I must goe along with her. But I excusing my selfe vpon Occasion of a present dispatch which I was to make vnto his Maiestie: The Dutches of Uantedor who followed her came to mee and said I must not refuse her wherevpon leading her by the Arme according to the manner of that Countrey; The Princesse of Conte offended that I had denied her that Ciuillity which I had yeilded to another tooke mee of after she had demaunded the Consent of the Dutches, But the Queene then also staying I left the Princesse and with all due humility went to the Queene and led her by the Arme. Walking thus to a place in the garden where some Oreng Trees grew and here discoursing with her Maiestie bare headed some small shott fell on both our heads The occasion whereof was this: The King being in the Garden and shooting at a Bird in the Aire (which hee did with much perfection) The descent of his shott fell just vpon vs; The Queene was much startled herewith. When I coming nearer to her demaunded whether shee had receiued any harme To which shee saying noe and therewith taking two or three small pelletts from her haire It was thought fitt to send a gardner to the King to tell him that her Maiestie was there and that hee should shoote noe more that way, which was no sooner heard among the Nobles that attended him, but many of them leaving him came to the Queen and Ladies, among whom was Monsieur le Grand who finding the Queen still discoursing with me stole behind her, and letting fall gently some comfetts he had in his pockett upon the Queens hair, gave her occasion to apprehend that some shot had fallen on her againe; Turning hereupon to Monsieur le Grand, I said that I marvelled that so old a Courtier as he was could find no means to entertain Ladies but by making them afraid. But the Queen shortly after returning to her Lodging, I took my leave of her and so came home. All which passage I have thought fit to set down, the accident above mentioned being so strange, that it can hardly be parellel'd.

It fell out one day that the Prince of Conde coming to my house, some speech happ'ned concerning the King my Master, in whom though he acknowledged much learning knowledge, Clemency, and divers other Vertues, yet he said he had heard that the King was much given to Cursing, I answered that it was one of his Gentlenesses, but the Prince demanding how Cursing could be a Gentleness, I replied yes, For though he could punish men himself, yet he left them to God to punish, which defence of the King my Master was afterwards much celebrated in the French Court.

Monsieur de Luines continuing still the Kings Favorite, advised him to War against his Subjects of the reform'd Religion in France, saying he would neither be a great Prince as long as he suffered so Puissant a Party to remaine within his Dominions, nor could justly stile himself the most Christian King, as long as he permitted such Hereticks to be in that great number they were, or to hold those strong Places which by publick Edict were assigned to them, and therefore that he should extirpate them as the Spaniards Had done the Moors, who are all banished into other Countreys as we may find in their Histories; This Counsell though approved by the Young King was yet disliked by other Grave and Wise Persons about him, and particularly by the Chancellor Sillery and the President Jannin, who thought better to have a Peace which had two Religions than a War which had none. Howbeit the Designe of Luines was applauded not only by the Jesuit Party in France, but by some Princes and other Martial Persons[1], insomuch that the Duke of Guise coming to see mee one day, said that they should never be happy in France, 'till those of the Religion were rooted out, I answer'd that I wondred to hear him say so, and the Duke demanding why, I replied that whensoever Those of the Religion were put down, the turn of the Great Persons and Governors of Provinces of that Kingdome would be next; and that though the present King were a good Prince, yet that their Successors may be otherwise, and that men did not know how soon Princes might prove Tyrants when they had nothing to fear; which Speech of mine was fatal, since those of the Religion were no sooner reduced into that weak condition in which now they are, but the Governors of Provinces were brought lower, and curbed much in their Power and Authority, And the Duke of Guise first of them all, so that I doubt not but my words were well remembred. Howsoever the War now went on with much fervor, neither could I diswade it, though using according to the Instructions I had from the King my Master many Arguments for that purpose. I was told often, that if the Reformation in France had been like that in England, where they observed we retained the Hierarchy together with decent Rights and Ceremonies in the Church as also Holidays in the memory of Saints, Musick in Churches, and divers other Testimonies both of Glorifying God and giving Honor and reward to Learning, they could much better have tolerated it; But such a Rash and Violent Reformation as theirs was, ought by no means to be approved, whereunto I answered, that though the Causes of departing from the Church of Rome were taught and delivered by many sober and modest Persons, yet that the Reformation in great part was acted by the Common People, whereas ours began at the Prince of State, and therefore was more moderate, which Reason I found did not displease them; I added further then that the Reform'd Religion in France would easily enough admit an Hierarchy, if they had sufficient means among them to maintaine it, and that if their Churches were as fair as those which the Roman Catholicks had, they would use the more decent sorts of Rites and Ceremonies, and together like well of Organs and Quires of Singers rather than make a Breach or Schism on that Occasion, as for Holidays I doubted not but the Principal Persons and Ministers of their

Religion would approve it much better than the common People, who being Labourers and Artizens for the most part had the Advantages for many more days than the Roman Catholicks for getting their Living; Howsoever that those of the Religion had been good Cautions to make the Roman Catholick Priests if not better yet at least more wary in their Life and Actions; It being evident that since the Reformation began among those of the Religion, the Roman Catholicks had divers ways reformed themselves, and abated not only much of their Power they usurped over Laics, but were more pious and continent than formerly. Lastly that those of the Religion acknowledged solely the Kings Authority in Government of all Affairs, whereas the Other Side held the Regal Power not only inferior in divers points, but subordinate to the Papal, Nothing of which yet served to divert Monsieur de Luines, or the King from their Resolutions.

The King having now assembled an Army, and made some Progresse against those of the Religion, I had instruction sent me from the King my Master to mediate a Peace, and if I could not prevail therein, to use some such words as may both argue his Majesties Care of them of the Religion, and together to let the French King know, that he would not permit their total Ruin and extirpation; The King was now going to lay Siege to St. Iean d'Angely, when my Self was newly recovered of a Feaver at Paris, in which besides the help of many able Physitians, I had the Comfort of divers Visits from many Principal Grandees of France, and particularly the Princess of Conti, who would set by my Bedside two or three hours, and with her cheerfull discourse entertaine me though yet I was brought so low, that I could scarce return any thing by way of answer but thanks. The Command yet which I received from the King my master quickned me insomuch that by slow degrees I went into my Coach together with my Train towards St. Jean d'Angely, Being arrived within a smal distance of that Place I found by divers Circumstances that the Effect of my Negotiation had been discovered from England, and that I was not welcome thither; howbeit I having obtained an Audience from the King, I exposed what I had in charge to say to him, to which yet I received no other Answer but that I should go to Monsieur de Luines by whom I should know his Majesties Intention: Repairing thus to him I did find outwardly good Reception, though yet I did not know how cunningly he proceeded to betray and frustrate my Endeavors for those of the Religion. For hiding a Gentleman called Monsieur Arnaud[1] behind the hangings in his Chamber, who was then of the Religion but had promised a Revolt to the Kings Side, this Gentleman, as he himself confessed afterwards to the Earle of Carlisle, had in charge to relate unto those of the Religion, how litle help they might expect from me, when he should tell them the answers which Monsieur d'Luines made me: Sitting thus in a Chair before Monsieur d'Luines, he demanded the effect of my Business, I answered that the King my Master commanded me to mediate a Peace betwixt his Majesty and his Subjects of the Religion, and that I desired to do it in all those fair and equal Terms which might stand with the honor of France and the good Intelligence betwixt the Two Kingdoms, to which he returned this rude answer only, What hath the King your Master to do with our Actions? Why doth he meddle with our affairs? My Reply was that the King my Master ought not to give him an Account of the reason which induced him hereunto, and for me it was enough to obey him; howbeit if he did ask me in more Gentle Terms, I should do the best I could to give him Satisfaction, To which though he answered no more than the Word, Bien, or well: I pursuing my Instruction said, That the King my master according to the mutual Stipulation betwixt Henry the Fourth and himself, that the Survivor of Either of them should procure the Tranquility and Peace of the Others Estate, had sent this message, and that he had not only testified this his pious Inclination heretofore in the late Civil Wars of France But was desirous on this occasion also to show how much he stood affected to the good of that Kingdome, besides he hoped that when Peace was established here, that the French King might be more easily disposed to assist the Palatine who was an Ancient Friend and Allie of the French Crown. His Reply to this was, we will have none of your Advices; whereupon I said that I took those words for an answer, and was sorry only that they did not understand sufficiently the affection and good will of the King my Master, and that since they rejected it upon these Terms, I had in charge to tell him that we knew very well what we had to do; Luines seeming offended herewith said, Nous ne Vous craignons pas, or we are not affraid of You, I replied hereupon that if you had said you had not loved us, I should have believed You, but should have returned You another answer. In the mean while that I had no more to say than what I told him formerly, which was, that we knew very well what we had to do. This though somewhat less than was in my Instructions, so angered him, that in much Passion he said, Per Dieu si Vous n'eties Monsieur l'Ambassadeur, Ie Vous traitterois d'un autre sorte, by God if you were not Monsieur Ambassador, I would use you after another Fashion. My answer was that as I was an Ambassador so I was also a Gentleman, and therewithall laying my hand upon the Hilt of my sword told him there was that which should make him an answer, and so arose from my Chair. To which Monsieur de Luines made no reply, but arising likewise from his Chair offered civilly to accompany me to the door, but I telling him there was no occasion for him to use Ceremony after so rude an Entertainment, I departed from him; from thence Returning to my Lodging, I spent 3 or 4 days afterwards in seeing the manner of the French discipline in making approaches to Towns, at what time I remember that going in my Coach within Reach of Cannon, those in the Town imagining me to be an Enemy, made many shots against me, which so affrighted my Coachman that he Durst drive no farther, whereupon alighting I bid him put the horses out of danger; and notwithstanding many more shots made against me, went on foot to the Trenches, where one Seaton a Scotchman conducting me, shewed me their Works, in which I found little differing from the Low Countrey manner. Having satisfied my Self in this manner, I thought fit to take my Leave of the King being at Cognac, the City of St. Jean d'Angely being now surrendered unto him. Coming thus to a Village not far from Cognac about ten of the Clock at night, I found all the Lodgings possessed by Souldiers, so

that alighting in the Market Place, I sent my Servants to the Inns
to get some provision, who bringing me only Six Rye Loavs,
which I was doubtfull whether I should bestow on my Self and
Company or on my Horses. Monsieur de Ponts a French Nobleman
of the Religion attended with a brave Train, hearing of my being
there offer'd me Lodging in his Castle near adjoyning, I told him it
was a great Courtesie at that time, yet that I could not with my
Honor accept it since I knew it would indanger him, my business to
those Parts being in favour of those of the Religion, and the Chief
Ministers of State in France being Jealous of my holding intelligence
with him; Howbeit if he would procure me Lodging in the Town,
I should take it kindly. Whereupon sending his Servants round
about the Town, he found at last in the House of one of his Tenants
a Chamber, to which when he had conducted me, and together
gotten some little accomodations for my Self and horses, I desired
him to depart to his Lodging, he being then in a Place, which his
Enemies the Kings Souldiers had possessed: All which was not so
silently carried but that the said Nobleman was accused afterwards at
the French Court upon Suspicion of holding Correspondence with
me, whereof it was my Fortune to clear him.

Coming next day to Cognac the Mareschall de St. Geran, my
Noble friend privately met me and said I was not in a Place of Surety
there as having offended Monsieur de Luines who was the Kings
Favorite, desiring me withall to advise what I had to do, I told him
that I was in a place of Surety wheresoever I had my sword by my
side, and that I intended to demand Audience of the King, which
also being obtained, I found not so cold a Reception as I thought to
meet with; insomuch that I parted with his Majesty to all outward
appearance in very good Terms.

From hence returning to Paris shortly after, I found my Self welcome to all those Ministers of State there and Noble Men who either
envied the Greatness or loved not the Insolencies of Monsieur de
Luines. By whom also I was told that the said Luines had intended
to send a Brother of his into England with an Ambasy—the effect
whereof should be chiefly to complaine against me, and to obtain

that I should be repeal'd[1], and that he intended to relate the Passages betwixt us at St. Iean d'Angely in a much different manner from that I reported, and that he would charge me with giving the first offence. After thanks for this advertisement I told them my Relation of the business betwixt us in the manner I delivered was true, and that I would justifie it with my sword, At which they being nothing scandalized, wish'd me good Fortune.

The Ambassador into England following shortly after with a huge Train[2] in a sumptuous manner, and an Accusation framed against me, I was sent for home, of which I was glad, my Payment being so ill, that I was run far in debt with my Merchants, who had assisted me now with 3 or 4000 l. more than I was able at the present to discharge. Coming thus to the Court, the Duke of Buckingham who was then my Noble Friend informed me at large of the Objections represented By the French Ambassador; to which when I had made my defence in the manner above related, I added that I was ready to make good all that I had said, with my sword, and shortly after I did in the presence of his Majesty and the Duke of Buckingham humbly desire Leave to send a Trumpet to Monsieur de Luines to offer him the Combate[3] upon terms that past betwixt us; which was not permitted, otherwise than that they would take my offer into Consideration. Howsoever Notice being publickly taken of this my desire, much occasion of speech was given, every man that heard thereof much favouring me, but the Duke of Luines death[4] following shortly after, the business betwixt us was ended, and I commanded to return to my former charge in France; I did not yet presently go as finding much difficulty to obtaine the moneys due to me from the Exchequer, and therewith, as also by my own Revenues, to satisfie my Creditors in France. The Earl of Carlisle this while being imployed Extraordinary Ambassador to France[5] brought home a Confirmation of the Passages betwixt Monsieur de Luines and my Self, Monsieur d'Arnaud who stood behind the hangings as is above related, having verified all I said, insomuch that the King my Master was well satisfied of my Truth.

Having by this time cleared all my Debts, when demanding new

Instructions from the King my Master, the Earl of Carlile brought me this message, that his Majesty had that experience of my Abilities and Fidelity, that he would give me no Instructions, but leave all things to my discretion, as knowing I would proceed with that Circumspection, as I should be better able to discerne upon emergent occasions what was fit to be done, than that I should need to attend directions from hence, which besides that they would be slow, might perchance be not so propper or correspondent to the Conjuncture of the great affairs then in agitation, both in France and Germany and other parts of Christendome, and that these things therefore must be left to my Vigilancy, Prudence, and Fidelity: Whereupon I told his Lordship that I took this as a singular expression of the Trust his Majesty reposed in me; howbeit that I desired his Lordship to pardon me, if I said I had herein only received a great Power and Latitude to err, and that I durst not trust my Iudgment so far as that I would presume to answer for all events in such factious and turbulent times, and therefore again did humbly desire New Instructions, which I promised punctually to follow. The Earle of Carlile returning hereupon to the King brought me yet no other answer back than that I formerly mention'd, and that his Majesty did so much confide in me, that he would limit me with no other instructions, but refer all to my discretion, promising together that if Matters proceeded not as well as might be wisht, He would attribute the Default to any thing rather than to my not performing my Duty.

Finding his Majesty thus resolved, I humbly took leave of him and my Friends at Court, and went to Monsieur Savage, when demanding of him New Letters of Credit, his answer was he could not furnish me as he had before there being no limited Sum expressed there, but that I should have as much as I needed; To which though I answered that I had paid all, yet as Monsieur Savage replied that I had not paid it at the time agreed on, he said he could furnish me with a Letter only for three Thousand Pounds, and nevertheless that he was confident I should have more if I required it, which I found true, for I took up afterwards upon my Credit there as much More as made in the whole five or six Thousand Pounds.

Coming thus to Paris I found my Self much welcomed by all the Principal Persons, no body that I found there being either offended with the Passages betwixt me and Monsieur de Luines, or that were sorry for his Death, In which number the Queens Majesty seemed the most eminent Person, as one who long since had hated him. Whereupon also I cannot but remember this passage, That in an Audience I had one day from the Queen, I demanded of her how far she would have assisted me, with her good Offices against Luines. She replied that what cause soever she might have to hate him, either by reason or by force, they would have made her to be of his Side, to which I answered in Spanish, No ay feurce por las a reynas, There is no force for Queens, at which she smiled.

And now I began to proceed in all publick Affairs according to the Liberty with which the King my Master was pleased to honor me, confining my Self to no Rules but those of my own discretion: My negotiations in the mean while proving so successfull, that during the remainder of my stay there, His Majesty receiv'd much satisfaction concerning My Carriage, as finding I had preserved his Honor and Interest in all the great Affairs then emergent in France, Germany and other parts of Christendome; which work being of great concernment I found the easier, that his Majesties Ambassadors and Agents every where gave me perfect Intelligence of all that hapned within their Precincts: Insomuch that from Sir Henry Wotton his Majesties Ambassador in Venice who was a learned and Witty Gentleman, I receiv'd all the News of Italy, as also from Sir Isaak Wake who did more particularly acquaint me with the business of Savoy, Valentina,[1] and Switzerland; From Sir Francis Nethersole his Majesty's Agent in Germany and more particularly with the United Princes there, on the behalf of his Son in Law the Palatine or King of Bohemia, I receiv'd all the News of Germany: From Sir Dudley Carlton his Majestys Ambassador in the Low Countrys I receiv'd intelligence concerning all the Affairs of that State; and from Mr. William Trumball his Majesties Agent at Brussels, all the affairs on that side; And Lastly from Sir Walter Aston his Majestys Ambassador in Spain, and after him from the

Earle of Bristol and Lord Cottington I had intelligence from the Spanish Court; Out of all whose Relations being compared together, I found matter enough to direct my Iudgment in all publick proceedings: Besides in Paris I had the chief Intelligence which came to either Monsieur de Langherac the Low Countrey Ambassador or Monsieur Postek Agent for the United Princes in Germany, and Sigr. Contarini Ambassador for Venice, and Sigr. Guiscardi my particular Friend Agent for Mantoua, and Monsieur Gueretin Agent for the Palatine or King of Bohemia, and Monsieur Villers Agent for the Suisse, and Monsieur Ainorant Agent for Geneva, By whose means upon the Resultance of the Several Advertisements given me, I found what I had to do.

The Wars in Germany were now hot, when several French Gentlemen came to me for Recommendations to the Queen of Bohemia, whose service they desired to Advance, which also I perform'd as effectually as I could; Howbeit as after the Battle of Prague, the Imperial Side seemed wholy to prevaile, These Gentlemen had not the satisfaction expected. About this time The Duke de Crouy imployed from Brussells to the French Court coming to see me said by way of Rhodomontade, as though he would not speak of our Isles, Yet he saw all the rest of the World must bow under the Spaniard; To which I answered God be thanked they are not yet at that pass, or when they were they have this yet to comfort them, that at worst they should be but the same which you are now: which speech of mine being afterwards, I know not how, divulged, was much applauded by the French, as believing I intended that Other Countreys should be but under the same severe Government to which the Duke of Crouy and those within the Spanish Dominions were subject.

It hap'ned one day that the Agent from Brussells and Ambassador from the Low Countreys came to see me immediately one after the other, to whom I said familiarly that I thought that the Inhabitants of the Parts of the Seventeen Provinces which were under the Spaniards might be compared to Horses in a Stable, which as they were finely curried, drest, and fed, so they were well ridden also,

Spurred, and galled: And that I thought the Low-Countrey Men were like to Horses at Grass, which though they wanted so good keeping as the Other had, yet might leap, kick, and fling, as much as they would, which freedom of mine displeased neither: Or if the Low-Countrey Ambassador did think I had spoken a little too sharply, I pleas'd him afterwards when I continuing my discourse, I told him that the States of the United Provinces had within a Narrow Room shut up so much Warlicke Provision both by Sea and Land, and together demonstrated such courage upon all occasions, that it seem'd they had more need of Enemies than of Friends; which Compliment I found did please him.

About this time the French being jealous that the King my Master would match the Prince his Son with the King of Spain's Sister, and together relinquish his Alliance with France, My Self who did endeavour Nothing more than to hold all good intelligence betwixt both Crowns, had enough to do. The Count de Gondomor passing now from Spain into England came to see me at Paris about Ten of the Clock in the morning, when after some Complements, he told me that he was to go towards England the next morning, and that he desired my Coach to accompany him out of Town; I told him after a free and merry manner he should not have my Coach, and that if he demanded it, it was not because he needed Coaches, The Pope's Nuntio, the Emperors Ambassador, the Duke of Bavaria's Agent, and others having Coaches enough to furnish him but because he would put a Jealousie betwixt me and the French, as if I inclined more to the Spanish Side than to theirs: Gondomor then looking merrily upon me said, I will dine with you yet; I told him by his good favor he should not dine with me at that time, and that when I would entertain the Ambassador of so great a King as his, it should not be upon my Ordinary, but that I would make him a Feast worthy of so great a Person; Howbeit that he might see after what manner I lived, I desired some of my Gentlemen to bring his Gentlemen into the Kitchen, where after my usual manner were three Spits full of Meat, divers pots of boyled meat, and an Oven with Store of Pyes in it, and a dresser board covered with all manner of good fowle, and some Tarts, Pans with Tarts in them after the French manner; After which being conducted to another Room they were shewed a dozen or sixteen dishes of Sweetmeats, All which was but the Ordinary Allowance for my Table: The Spaniards returning now to Gondomor told him what good cheer they found, notwithstanding which I told Gondomor againe that I desired to be excused, if I thought this Dinner unworthy of him, and that when occasion were I should entertaine him after a much better manner; Gondomor hereupon coming near me, said he esteemed me much, and that he meant only to put a Trick upon me, which he found I had discover'd, and that he thought that an English man had not known how to avoid handsomely a Trick put upon him under shew of Civility; and that I ever should find him my friend and would do me all the good offices he could in England, which also he really perform'd, as the Duke of Lenox and the Earle of Pembrook confirm'd to me, Gondomor saying to them, that I was a man fit for Imployment, and that he thought Englishmen though otherwise able Persons, knew not how to make a denial handsomely, which yet I had done.

This Gondomor being an able Person and dexterous in his Negotiations, had so prevailed with King Iames that his Majesty resolved to pursue his Treaty with Spain, and for that purpose to send his Son Prince Charles in Person to conclude the Match; when after some debate whether he should go in Publick or Private manner, it was at last resolved, that He attended with the Marquis of Buckingham, and Sir Francis Cottington his Secretary, and Endimion Porter, and Mr. Grimes Gentleman of the Horse to the Marquis should pass in a disguised and private manner through France to Madrid; These five passing though not without some difficulty from Dover to Bulloigne where taking post Horses they came to Paris and lodged at an Inn in Rue St Jacques, where it was advised amongst them whether they should send for me to attend them; After some dispute, It was concluded in the Negative since (As one there objected) if I came alone in the Quality of a Private Person, I must go on foot through the Streets, and because I was a

Person generally known might be followed by some one or other, who would discover whither my private visit tended, besides that those in the Inn must needs take notice of my coming in that manner; On the other side if I came publickly with my usual Train, the Gentlemen with me must needs take notice of the Prince and Marquis of Buckingham, and consequently might divulge it, which was thought not to stand with the Prince's safety, who endeavour'd to keep his Iourney as secret as was possible. Howbeit the Prince spent the day following his Arrival in seeing the French Court and City of Paris without that any body did know his Person, but a maid that had sold Linnen heretofore in London, who seeing him pass by said, certainly this is the Prince of Wales, but withall suffered him to hold his way and presumed not to follow him. The next day after they took Post Horses and held there way towards Bayone a City Frontier to Spain.

The first notice that came to me was by one Andrews a Scotchman, who coming late the night preceding their departure, demanded whether I had seen the Prince, when I demanding what Prince, for said I, the Prince of Conde is yet in Italy, he told me the Prince of Wales, which yet I could not believe easily untill with many Oaths he affirm'd the Prince was in France, and that he had charge to follow his Highness, desiring me in the mean while on the part of the King my Master to serve his passage the best I could. This made me rise very early the next morning and go to Monsieur Puisieux Principal Secretary of State to demand present Audience. Puisieux hereupon intreated me to stay an hour since he was in bed, and had some earnest business to dispatch for the King his Master as soon as he was ready; I returned answer that I could not stay a minute, and that I desired I might come To his bedside, this made Puisieux rise and put on his Gown only and so came to the Chamber where I attended him. His first words to me were, I know your business as well as You, Your Prince is departed this morning post to Spain, adding further, that I could demand nothing for the security of his Passage, but it should be presently granted, concluding with these very words, Vous serez servi au point nomme, or you shall be

Louis XIII; oil painting by S. Vouet

Anne of Austria; oil painting by Rubens

Hugo Grotius; etching c. 1640

served in any particular you can name, I told him that his free offer had prevented the request I intended to make, and that because he was so principall a Minister of State I doubted not but what he had so nobly promised he would see punctually performed. As for the security of his passage, that I did not see what I could demand more, than that he would suffer him quietly to hold his way without sending after or interrupting him. He replied that the Prince not be interrupted though yet he could do no less than send to know what success the Prince had in his Iourney: I was no sooner return'd out of his chamber, but I dispatch't a Letter by post to the Prince to desire him to make all the hast he could out of France, and not to treat with any of the Religion in the way since his being at Paris was known, and that though the French Secretary had promised he should not be interrupted, yet that they would send after his Highness, and when he gave any occasion of Suspicion, might perchance detaine him. The Prince after some examination at Bione (which the Governour thereof did afterwards particularly relate to me) confessing that he did not know who the Prince was, held his way on to Madrid, where he and all his Company safely arrived; Many of the Nobility and others of the English Court being now desirous to see the Prince, did pass through France to Spain taking my house still in their way, by whom I acquainted his Highness in Spain how much it grieved me that I had not seen his Highness when he was in Paris, which occasioned his Highness afterwards to write a Letter to me wholly with his own hand and subscribe his name your Friend Charles, in which He did abundantly satisfie all the unkindness I might conceive on this occasion.

I shall not enter into a Narration of the passages occuring in the Spanish Court upon his Highness's Arrival thither, though they were well known to me for the most part, by the Information the French Queen was pleased to give me, who among other things told me that her Sister[1] did wish well unto the Prince; I had from her also intelligence of certaine Messages sent from Spain to the Pope, and the Popes Messages to them, whereof by her permission I did afterwards inform his Highness. Many Judgments were now made concerning the Event, which this Treaty of Marriage was likely to have; The Duke of Savoy said that the Prince's Iourney thither was, Un tiro di quelli Cavellieri antichi che andavano cosi per il Mondo a diffare li incanti, That it was a Trick of those ancient Knight Errands who went up and down the World after that manner to undoe Inchantments; for as that Duke did believe that the Spaniard did intend finally to bestow her on the Imperial House, he conceiv'd that he did only entertaine the Treaty with England, because he might avert the King my Master from Treating in any other Place and particularly in France; Howbeit by the Intelligence I received in Paris, which I am confident was very good, I am assured the Spaniard meant really at that time, though how the Match was broken, I list not here to relate, it being a more perplext and secret business than I am willing to insert into the Narration of my Life.

New Propositions being now made and other Counsells there-upon given, The Prince taking his Leave of the Spanish Court came to St. Anderos in Spain where shipping himself with his Train arrived safely at Portsmouth about the beginning of October 1623, the News whereof being shortly brought into France, the Duke of Guise came to me and said he found the Spaniards were not so able men as he thought, since they had neither married the Prince in their Country, nor done any thing to break his Match else where, I answered that the Prince was more dexterous than that any secret practice of theirs could be put upon him; And as for Violence I thought the Spaniard durst not offer it.

The War against those of the Religion continuing still in France, Pere Segnerand Confessor to the King made a Sermon before his Majesty upon the Text, That we should forgive our Enemies, upon which Argument having said many good things, he at last distinguished forgivenesses, and said, We were indeed to forgive our Enemies but not the Enemies of God, such as were Hereticks, and particularly those of the Religion, and that his Majesty, as the most Christian King ought to extirpate them wheresoever they could be found: This particular being related to me, I thought fit to go to the Queen Mother without further Ceremony, for she gave me leave to come to her chamber whensoever I would, without demanding Audience, and to tell her that though I did not usually intermedle with matters handled within their Pulpits, Yet because Pere Segnerand who had charge of the Kings Conscience had spoken so violently against those of the Religion, that his doctrine was not limited only to France, but might extend it self in its Consequences beyond the Seas even to the Dominions Of the King my Master; I could not but think it very unreasonable, and the rather, that as her Majesty well knew, that a Treaty of Mariage betwixt our Prince and the Princess her Daughter was now began for which reason I could do no less than humbly desire that such doctrines as these henceforth might be silenced by some discreet Admonition, she might please to give to Pere Segnerand, or others that might speak to this purpose: The Queen though She seemed very willingly to hear me, yet handled the business so, that Pere Segnerand was together inform'd who had made this complaint against him, whereupon also he was so distemper'd, that by one Monsieur Gaellac a Provencall his own Countryman he sent me this Message; that he knew well who had accused him to her Majesty, and that he was sensible thereof, that he wisht me to be assured, that wheresoever I was in the World, he would hinder my Fortune. The answer I returned by Monsieur Gaellac was, That nothing in all France but a Fryar or a Woman durst have sent me such a Message.

Shortly after this coming again to the Queen Mother, I told her that what I said concerning Pere Segnerand was spoken with a good intention, and that my Words were now discovered to him in that manner, that he sent me a very affronting Message, adding after a merry fashion these words, that I thought Segnerand so malicious that his malice was beyond the malice of Women; The Queen being a litle startled hereat, sayed a moy femme et parler ainsi, to me a Woman and say so? I replied gently, Ie parle a vôtre Majeste comme Reyne et non pas comme femme, I speak to your Majesty as a Queen and not as a Woman, and so took my leave of her. What Pere Segnerand did afterwards in way of performing his threat I know not, but sure I am that had I been Ambitious of Worldly greatness

I might have often remembered his words, though as I ever loved my Book and a private life more than any busie Preferments, I did frustrate and render vain his greatest power to hurt me.

My book De Veritate prout distinguitur a Revelations verisimili, possibili, et à falso, having been begun by me in England, and formed there in all its principal Parts, was about this time finished;[1] all the spare hours which I could get from my Visits and Negotiations being imployed to perfect this work, which was no sooner done, but that I communicated it to Hugo Grotius that great scholar,[2] who having escaped his Prison in the Low Countreys, came into France and was much welcomed by me and to Monsieur Tieleners also, one of the greatest Scholars of his time, who after they had perused it and given it more commendations than is fit for me to repeat, exhorted me earnestly to print and publish it; Howbeit as the frame of my whole Book was so different from any thing which had been written heretofore, I found I must either renounce the Authority of All that had written formerly concerning the Method of finding out Truth, and consequently insist upon my own way, or hazard my Self to a general Censure concerning the whole argument of my Book; I must confess it did not a litle animate me, That the Two great Persons above mention'd did so highly value it, yet as I knew it would meet with much opposition, I did consider whether it was not better for me a while to suppress it: being thus doubtfull in my Chamber one fair day in the Summer, my Casement being opened towards the South, the Sun shining clear and no wind stirring, I took my Book de Veritate in my hand, and kneeling on my knees devoutly said these words,

O Thou Eternal God Author of that Light which now shines upon me, and Giver of all inward illuminations, I do beseech Thee of thy infinite Goodness to pardon a greater request than a Sinner ought to make; I am not satisfied enough whether I shall publish This Book De Veritate, if it be for thy Glory, I beeseech thee give me some Signe from Heaven, if not, I shall suppress it.

I had no sooner spoken these words, but a Loud though yet Gentle noise came from the Heavens (for it was like nothing on

Earth) which did so comfort and cheer me, that I took my Petition
as granted, and that I had the Signe I demanded, whereupon also I
resolved to print my Book: This (how strange soever it may seem)
I protest before the Eternal God is true, neither am I any way super-
stitiously deceived herein, since I did not only clearly hear the
Noise, but in the Serenest Skye that ever I saw being without all
cloud did to my thinking see the Place from whence it came.

And now I sent my Book to be printed in Paris at my own Cost
and Charges without suffering it to be divulged to others than to
such as I thought might be worthy Readers of it, though afterwards
reprinting it in England, I not only dispersed it among the Prime
Scholars of Europe, but was sent to not only from the nearest but
Furtherst parts of Christendome to desire the sight of my Book, for
which they promised any thing I should desire by way of return,
but hereof more amply in its place.

The Treaty of a Match with France continuing still, It was thought
fit for the concluding thereof that the Earle of Carlile and the Earle
of Holland should be sent Extraordinary Ambassadors to France.[1]

Textual Notes

THESE NOTES list only those variants or manuscript alterations which materially affect the meaning of the text. But because the primary source for the printed text is a manuscript with corrections in the author's hand I have included many of Lord Herbert's changes and in some cases original passages later struck out, for they often help clarify his intent.

Likewise I have listed only the most important of the variants between the MSS. and the printed editions.

ABBREVIATIONS

A	the scribe who copied *AuW*
AuE	the original MS. in the hand of Rowland Evans
AuLee	the edition by Sir Sidney Lee (1886; rev. 1906)
AuW	the derivative MS. which Walpole used as his source
Au1764	the first edition, by Horace Walpole
B	the editor who annotated *AuW* in light pencil
C	the reader who annotated *AuW* in ink
E	Rowland Evans, Lord Herbert's secretary
H	Lord Herbert
s.o.	struck out; strike out
~	key words in text
∧	omission

References are to page and line:
1.*AuW is copy text*
8.9 church] *AuW. What seems a semi-colon to a careless reader is a comma following* church *above which appears a small stain. That Walpole printed it as a semi-colon is evidence of his setting type from AuW* 8.27 went to the] *Au1764;* ~∧~ *AuW.* 9.28 After] *AuE begins* 9.30 aboue] about *AuW*

9.32 time] *om. AuW* 10.27 before] to *AuW* 10.35 called————] *blank in both MSS., apparently left to be filled in when Herbert recalled or found the name* 11.19 Afternoone] morning *AuW* 11.19 Infancy *AuW*: infantry *AuE; error probably from mishearing. AuW corr. to* Infancy *by A* 11.25 first] furtherest *AuW* 11.27 but for] but from *Au1764* 12.8 VITA] *AuW has a longer version:*

PRIMA fuit quondam genitali semine Vita
Procurasse suas dotes, ubi Plastica Virtus
Gestiit, et vegeto molem perfundere Succo,
Externamq; suo formam cohibere recessu,
Dum conspirantes possint accedere causae,   5
Et totum tuto licuit proludere foetum.

    Altera materno tandem succrevit in arvo,
Exiles spumans ubi spiritus induit Artus,
Exertusq; simul miro sensoria textu
Cudit, et hospitium menti non vile paravit,   10
Quae Caelo delaps suas mox inde capessat
Partes, et sortis tanquam praesaga futurae
Corrigat ignavum pondus, nec inutile sistat.

    Tertia nunc agitur, qua Scena recluditur ingens,
Cernitur et festum Caeli, Terraeq; Theatrum;   15
Congener et species, rerum variataq; forma;
Et circumferri, motu proprioq vagari
Contigit, et lege aeternaq; fadera mundi
Visere, et assiduo redeuntia sidera cursu.   20
Unde etiam vitae causas, nexumq; tueri
Fas erat et summum longe praesciscere Numen;
Dum varios mire motus contemperet orbis,
Et Pater, et Dominus, Custos, & Conditor idem
Audit ubiq; Deus; Quid ni modo QUARTA sequatur?   25
Sordibus excussis cum mens jam purior instat,
Auctaq; doctrinis variis, viruteq; pollens
Intendit vires, magis et sublimia spirat,
Et tacitus cordi stimulus suffigitur imo,
Ut velit heic quisquam sorti superesse caducae,   30
Expetiburq; status faelicior ambitiosis,
Ritibus, et sacris, et cultu religioso,
Et nova successit melioris conscia Fati

Spes superis haerens, toto perfusaq; Caelo,
Et sese sancto demittit Numen Amori,   35
Et data Caelestis non fallax Tessera Vitae,
Cumʹq; Deo licuit non uno jure pacisci,
Ut mihi seu servo reddatur debita merces,
Filius aut bona adire paterna petam, mihi sponso
Sit fidei Numen; mox hanc sin exuo vitam,   40
Compos jam factus melioris, tum simul uti
Jure meo cupiam liber, meq; asserit inde
Ipse Deus (cujus non terris Gratia tantum,
Sed Caelis prostat) Quid ni modo QUINTA sequatur,
Et SEXTA, et quicquid tandem spes ipsa requirat?   45

Immediately following Vita *in Au W:*

ED VITA CAELESTI CONJECTURA

Toto lustratus Genio mihi graulor ipsi,
Fati securus, dum nec terroribus ullis
Dejicior, tacitos condo vel corde dolores,
Sed laetus mediis aerumnis transigo vitam,
Invitisq; malis (quae terras undiq; cingunt)   5
Ardenti virtute viam super aethera quaerens,
Proxima Caelestis praecepi praemia vitae,
Ultima praetento, divino mixus amore,
Quo simul exuperans creperae ludibria sortis,
Barbara vesani linquo consortia Saeĉli   10
Auras infernas defflans, spiransq; supernas,
Dum sanctis memet totum sic implico flammis,
Hiisce ut suffultus penetrem laquearia Caeli,
Atq; novi late speculer magnalia Mundi,   15
Et notas animas, proprio jam lumine pulchras
Invisam, Super̂umq; choros, mentesq; beatas,
Quêis aveam mincere ignes, ac vincula sacra,
Atq; vice alterna transire in gaudia, Caelum
Quae dederit cunctis, ipsis aut indita nobis,   20
Vel quae communi voto sacire licebit.
Ut Deus interea cumulans sua praemia, nostrum
Augeat inde decus, proprioq; illustret amore,
Nec Caeli Caelis desint, aeternave Vitae

Saecula, vel Saecĉlis nova gaudia, qualia totum   25
Aevum nec minuat, nec terminat Infinitum.
His major desit nec gratia Numinis alma,
Quae miris variata modis haec gaudia crescant,
Excipiatq; statum quemvis faelicior alter;
Et quae nec sperare datur sint praestita nobis,   30
Nec nisi sola capit quae mens divina, superfint;
Quae licet ex sese sint perfectissima longe,
Ex nobis saltem mage condecorata videntur:
Cum segnes animas, caelum quas indit ab ortu,
Exacuat tantum labor ac industria nostra;   35
Ac demum poliat doctrina, et moribus illis,
Ut redeant pulchrae, dotem caeloq; reportent:
Quum simùl arbitriis usi, mala pellimus illa,
Quae nec vel pepulit caelum, vel pelleret olim,
Ex nobis ita fit jam gloria Numinis ingens,   40
Auctior, in caelos quoq; gloria nostra redundat,
Et quae virtuti sint debita praemia tandem
Vel Numen solito reddunt faelicius ipsum.
Amplior unde simul redhibetur Gratia nobis,
Ut vel pro voto nostro jam singula cedant.   45
Nam si libertas chara est per amaena locorum
Conspicua innumeris Caelis discurrere fas est,
Deliciasq; loci cujusvis carpere passim.
Altior est animo si contemplatio fixa est,
Cuncta adaperta patent nobis jam scrinia Caeli,   50
Arcanasq; Dei rationes nosse juvabit:
Hujus sin repetat quisquam consortia saecli,
Mox agere in terris, ac procurare licebit
Res heic humanas, et justis legibus uti:
Sin mage caelesti jam delectamur amore,   55
Solvimur in flammas, quae se lambuntq; foventq;
Mutuo, & impliciti sanctis ardoribus, una
Surgimus amplexi, copula junctiq; tenaci,
Partibus, et toto miscemur ubiq; vicissim;
Ardoresq; novos accendit Numinis ardor.   60
Sin laudare Deum lubeat, nos laudat et ipse,
Concinit Angelicusq chorus, modulamine suavi

Personat et caelum, prostant et publica nobis
Gaudia, et eduntur passim spectacula laeta;
Fitq; theatralis quasi Caeli machina tota.   65
Hanc mundi molem sin vis replicaverit ingens
Numinis, atq; novas formas exculpserit inde
Dotibus ornatas alijs, magis atq; capaces;
Nostras mox etiam formas renovare licebit,
Et dotes sensusq; alios assumere, tandem   70

13.5 That Vis Plastica] That this Plastica *AuW* 13.6 or Formatrix] *supra,*
H. *Evans had written* of her Matrix (*aural error*) 13.6 framed] formed
AuW 13.24 that did] that it did *Au1764* 13.28 Facultyes (though] faculties
therefore tho *AuW* 13.30 or long] or remain long *AuW* 14.2 schoolemaster in the] *orig.* schoolemaster then in my (*dictation change*) 14.5 That at
the end . . . soe much] *om. AuW* 14.10 or . . . Trick] *om. AuW* (*example
of A's frequent attempt at clarification*) 14.20 I *AuW*] in *AuE* 15.1 found . . .
Coller] *supra*; did admire him so, *s.o.*, H. 15.7 remitt . . . Passion,] *supra*;
digest much of his Choller, *s.o.*, H. 15.34 elder] eldest *AuW* 16.22
Vroxeter) that] *om. AuW* 16.23 me. Not] me, I espoused her. Not *AuW*
16.26 a due . . . inclined] *supra*, H. *The passage s.o. reads* nothing that might
avert mee to those Inticements to which youth is subiect. 16.32 whereof
. . . day] *om. AuW* 17.10 deboist] debauchery *AuW*; *the copyist for AuW
was puzzled by the original and left space, but* debauchery *was longer than he
anticipated and the word is cramped.* 17.21 herbes] as Milium Solis saxifragia
added interlinearly in AuW by unknown hand 17.31 as also . . . Advice]
*orig. in AuE but s.o. by an unknown editor; I include the original reading because
AuW has the passage verbatim and because the unaltered lines which follow make
little sense if it is omitted.* 18.6 say . . . more] *supra*; much enlarge my selfe,
s.o., H. 18.15 Infancy, otherwise] infancy Since otherwise *AuW* 18.30 and
vnvsuall] than usual *AuW* (*suggests that part of AuW was written from dictation*)

19.9 imitate] *supra* (*orig.* doe *which was s.o. and* follow *written in*): follow
AuW (*suggests source transcribed before AuE final correction*) 19.16 either] *om.
AuW* 19.33 show] *supra*; teach, *s.o.*, H. 19.34 sophismes] *supra*, H. 20.17
requisite] fit *AuW* (*earlier reading from AuE*) 20.29 demonstration it is *AuW*:
∼∧∼ *AuE* 20.34 could] *AuE hiatus; AuW resumed as copy-text.* 22.1 I said]
om. Au1764 23.6 Hipocrates.] *AuE resumed as copy-text.* 23.11 or] *added in
left margin,* E; *om. AuW.* 23.18 cutt] cull *AuW* 23.19 of the Herbes there]
om. AuW 23.33 is daunger] is Less danger *AuW* 24.10 pin] *om. AuW*;

Disease *Au1764* 24.10 she made it. . . . Soule.] *orig.* she hath made the Soule Close prisoner to the Body: to have made it *AuW* 24.24 as *AuW*: is *AuE* 24.32 life by vertue] Life in vertue *AuW* 26.2 those who are magistrates and much your superiors] those that are much your Superiors, who are Magistrates, etc. *AuW* 26.23 3 *AuW*: Thirdly *AuE*: 26.32 and being that] *om. AuW* 27.12 on *AuW*: and *AuE*. (*AuW first copies faithfully but* and *was s.o. and* on *added supra by B*) 27.21 them.] 8 *lines s.o. by heavy scribbling:* . . . them there being noe man that either in Words prayers Rites and Ceremonyes can soe truly either serve God or doe good to his Neighbour as in a Constant practice of these Seasonable vertues alone [*unclear*] with which also I am confident even the highest vertue would be impertinent and troublesome not onely to mans selfe but to others 27.28 not . . . illustrated] but underset and holpen a little *AuW* (*reading copied from AuE before final correction*) 28.22 And certainly] *om. AuW* 28.33 written of] written a book of *AuW*

29.14 that when a] that a *AuW* 29.21 that] who *AuW* 29.22 then himselfe *AuW*; *AuE has* then abler then himself: than abler *s.o. in AuW by B* 29.24 necessary.] *The passage beginning* Concerning Religion *and continuing to 31.17, any other. here printed as part of the text for the first time. Omitted from AuW and all subsequent editions; printed by R.I. Aaron in MLR XXXVI (1941), 192–3* 32.8 either they should] either should *Au1764* 32.22 as he shall . . . thrust] *om. Au1764* 32.23 how to *AuW*: how *AuE* 32.24 Adversary] enemy *AuW* 32.31 dexterously] *supra*; happily *s.o.*, H. 32.32 since . . . Fencing] *supra*, H. 32.35 affording] giving *AuW* (*incorr. reading of AuE*) 33.11 this to bee] is to be *AuW* 33.20 retyring] returning *AuW* 34.30 still more] still some more *AuW* 34.30 this] his *AuW* 34.35 after which] which being done *AuW* 35.22 If] *supra*; yet if you bring *s.o.*, H. 36.2 men] Gentlemen *AuW* 36.16 Relation] Narration *AuW* 36.17 of about] betwixt *AuW* 36.17 and] or *AuW* 36.30 youngest] younger *AuW* 37.12 gaue mee her] gave her *AuW* 37.21 Order, wherevpon I] Order, I *AuW* 38.4 Romances] *orig.* Romans 38.5 day they are to] day to *AuW* 38.26 money] gift *AuW* (*incorr. reading from AuE*) 38.29 I] and *AuW* 39.5 bed.] *A space of about eight MS. lines has been left before the abrupt resumption with the narrative of the Gunpowder Plot. The passage which follows, to p. 40.14, has not before been included as part of the* Autobiography. 39.23 by the falling . . . fire] *supra*; by setting fire casually *s.o.*, E. 40.28 sonnes] Son *AuW* 41.18 loyally] honestly *AuW*

42.11 going from] going one evening from *AuW* (*uncorr. reading from AuE*)
42.25 ouertooke] *supra*; seased on *s.o.*, H. 42.31 answered *AuW*: *altered to*
answering *in AuE* 42.32 soe I conducted] so conducted *AuW* 42.35 seem-
ing] seeing him *AuW* 43.10 vpon the same poynt] *supra*, H; *om. AuW*
43.15 heir to the said] *This passage which concludes at 43.20 . . . thought*
fitt is missing from AuW; the copyist purposely omitted it, altering to maintain
the semblance of continuity. AuW reads: . . . Heir sent him a challenge, which
to this day he never answered, and would . . . *Between* Heir *and* sent *C*
inserted a carat with the note here seems to be at least a line wanting. *Au1764*
prints a similar notice. In Walpole's Letters (ed. Cunningham. iv, 275) *appears*
a nearly correct version of the passage with the statement that this paper was given
to me in 1789, by W. Seward, Esq., who told me it was copied by Mr.
Ingram from the original MS., which MS., I suppose is the copy of the
Memoires of which I had heard, but never saw. The passage was not in
the copy which Lord Powis lent me, and from which this edition was
printed. *AuLee silently alters the passage.* 43.23 but that . . . Newport] *supra*,
H. 43.35 Vanachly] Hanachly *AuW* 44.6 seeing] perceiving *AuW* 44.15
he did] was done *AuW* 44.27 Knighthood. For] Knighthood; since *AuW*
44.30 noe not] so that *AuW* 44.31 occasion quarrelled] occasion given
AuW 44.35 had occasion to drawe] yet drew *AuW* 44.35 sake, as] sake,
singly, as *AuW* 45.4 de] in *AuW* 45.8 were *AuW*: *om. AuE* 45.12 not]
nor *AuW* 45.13 much] great *AuW* 45.28 had neuer gott] will neither have
got *AuW* 45.29 you *AuW*: him *AuE* (*uncorrected dictation*) 45.30 exaumple,
It] example at least of the former part, it *AuW* 46.5 the one] that *AuW*
(*the beginning of a series of variations which occur because AuW's source was*
copied from AuE before it was completely revised) 46.5 much] that *AuW* 46.11
wee] are *AuW* 46.13 fight cruelly with] fight with *AuW* 46.15 when
overtaken was easily] when he were overtaken easily *AuW* 46.20 turnd
head] turned his head *Au1764* 46.21 against them] against our Dogs *AuW*
46.22 dangerously when I] dangerously I *AuW* 46.23 yet . . . enter]
entring *AuW* 43.24 could perce him] should be *AuW* 46.27 returned on
foote with] returned with *AuW* 46.34 charge] turn upon *AuW*

47.5 sent] presented *AuW* 47.5 who found] and found *AuW* 47.7 And
Thus I] Thus having *AuW* 47.13 its Course] *om. AuW* 47.17 strong Castle]
orig. sumptuous Castle, E. 47.18 founded] furnish'd *AuW* 47.24 yet . . .
Castle] *orig.* yet was not this in my opinion the chiefe Glory of this strong
and stately house (*alteration by E; dictation change*) 47.31 meete (*correcting*

overtake)] meet or overtake *AuW* 47.31 as] they *AuW* 47.33–48.6
Both . . . home] *Nine lines added by E to left margin of AuE replacing two
lines s.o.*: And particularly when I was Ambassedor in the tyme of his
Sonne the late Duke of Montmorency 48.9 fifth the greate *AuW*: fifth
theire greate *AuE* 48.25 Chantily] St. Ilee *AuW* 49.4 did litle] did not a
little *AuW* 49.15 lodged in] received to *AuW* 49.27 wont] *AuE hiatus, pp.
73–84 wanting.* 51.23 receiv'd, bid] receiv'd, I bid *Au1764* 54.23 Crosse]
Crofts *AuW* 58.29 that I] *AuE resumes* 59.31 stayd a while] past some
time *AuW* 59.34 My Lord] the Lord *AuW* 60.20 Aeres] *AuW consistently
alters to* Ayres 60.21 Copy . . . afterwards] *AuW alters this heavily corrected
passage to* Copy of my Picture from Larkin, gave it to Mr. Isaac the Painter
in Blackfriars, and desired him to draw it in little after his manner, which
being done she 60.28 euer] either *AuW* 60.34 confesse no] confess I think
no *AuW* 61.17 the tyme] her time *AuW* 62.7 should] did *AuW* 62.9 to
Assassinate] *supra*; against *s.o.*, E? 62.15 with purpose] on purpose *AuW*
62.30 men together assaulting] men assaulting *AuW* 62.32 the best] as well
as *AuW* 63.19 would] could *AuW* 64.17 and weapons] and his weapons
AuW 64.27 left him] left in him *AuW* 64.35 Uille] *AuW misreads as* Hill
65.6 the Counsell] the Privy Counsell *AuW* 65.31 and theire] and all
their *AuW*

66.1 fellowes] Followers *AuW* 66.27 Ventedour *AuLee*: Antedor *AuE*
67.7 which . . . but] *supra*; I hearing this *s.o.*, H. 67.8 the middle] his
middle *AuW* 67.14 turned] returned *AuW* 68.10–12 The Low Countrey
. . . Coach] *heavily corrected. orig.* His Army being now ready went into
the feild his Excellency commanding a Waggoneer which Cost six shillings
a day to be allowed mee at the Charge of the States both for Carriage of
my Clothes and Armes and with providing Forredge. taking my selfe
along with him sometymes in his Coach (*H's alterations*) 68.14 towards]
near *AuW* 68.21 part.] *Following* part E *wrote* and those who for vnhand-
somenes could not justly feare Ravishment *but immediately stuck it out.*
68.31 his Pioners] *orig.* his Spioners 69.1 the Enemie appeared that] Spinola
with his Army appeared *AuW* (*alteration of AuE's orig.* Spinola with his
Army were come to the Place) 69.7 noe Enemy shew] no shew of the
Enemy *AuW* 69.8 for anything] as *AuW* 69.14 sword and] sword in my
hand *AuW* 69.28 the best] as well as *AuW* 69.34 motions. Nothing]
motions. For the rest nothing *AuW* 70.1 to *AuW*] *om. AuE; incomplete
correction* 70.8 speake;] *AuE hiatus; pp. 101–4 wanting; AuW becomes the*

copy text 70.12 him together to] him to *Au1764* 72.25 betwixt that and the]
betwixt the *Au1764* 72.32 to Kysarswert] Rysarswert *AuW* 73.10 shewed]
AuE resumed as copy-text 73.13 Tyme; we *AuW*] tyme, came *AuE* 73.20
voyce, I sayd: ∼∧∧∼ *AuE* 73.29 beautified on all the] *orig.* Couered
all on the 74.3 brought] bred *AuW* 74.24 loued euery] *supra*; hated noe
s.o., E. 74.26 Now] And *AuW* 74.32 Acts] Arts *AuW* 75.1 When] which
being done *AuW* 75.10 where . . . awhile] *om. AuW* 75.22 friend in
England) being] friend I know not *AuW* (*uncorr. reading from AuE*) 75.25
From] After I had stayed a while, from *AuW* 75.33 because] as *AuW* 76.32
when . . . letter] *heavily corrected, it stands in the MS. reading* When Counte
Scarnafigi came to mee from the duke Ouertaking mee brought mee a
letter. *AuW emends to* when the Count Scarnafigi came to me from the
Duke and brought a Letter. *AuLee follows AuW but emends to* Scarnifissi
throughout 77.25 servants] officers *AuW* 77.27 which for more expedition of which *Au1764* 77.30 vpon Condition] which I granted on Condition *AuW* 77.34 rayse] pay *AuW* 77.35 above nominated] *supra; orig.*
I should leavy *s.o.*

78.5 hcad yet] head or person yet *AuW* 78.13 came to] came near *AuW*
78.22 tis ods but] perhaps *AuW* 78.31 Saying] My answer was *AuW* 78.32
it for] it all my Life for *AuW* 79.1 Course Faire] coarse Cheer *AuW*
79.12 rest there for two] rest two *AuW* 79.22 heyre] air *AuW* 80.2 Slashes
and] Slashes, from the shoulder and sleeves unto the foot and *AuW* (*gratui-
tous addition*) 80.10 onely did refresh] alone did somewhat refresh *AuW*
80.23 well as] well on my part as *AuW* 80.25 him] them *Au1764* 80.29
Attendance] Attendants *AuW* 80.34 Turin, I] Turin? to which I *AuW*
81.4 hee] this man *Au1764* 81.11 mee faire] me very fair *Au1764* 81.13
brought] conducted *AuW* 81.20 as dismissed] as he dismissed *AuW* 81.24
thee] you *AuW* 81.30 Well, said hee] *om. Au1764* 81.32 returning to the
AuW: ∼∧∼ *AuE* 82.4 Charity] Civility *AuW* 82.11 before . . . Company]
om. Au1764 82.23 The Gouernor . . . returned] *orig.* Turning backe thus
an humble Obeysance to his Lady and soe returned. 84.16 assez] asser
AuW 84.18 Gouernor I demaunded *Au1764, Lee*] ∼∧ ∼ *AuE, AuW* 84.21
ended. Wherevpon after] ended, after *AuW* 84.23 and my selfe] *om. AuW*
84.27 goe to] *om. Au1764* 85.11 at length] *AuE hiatus; AuW becomes copy-
text* 85.15 St. Islands] Sandilands *Au1764* 86.10 to him] to come to him
Au1764 87.16 Kings forgiveness] King ∼ *AuW* 89.12 have been] be
Au1764 90.27 stayd: staye *AuW* 91.13 of one] *om. Au1764* 95.31 Carew]

Caage *AuW; emended Lee.*   97.6 betweene] *AuE resumed as copy-text;* betwixt *AuW*   97.23 it] them *AuW*   97.27 Ambassedours] *AuW here is misnumbered, skipping from p. 127 to 148*   98.5 of money] *om. AuW*   99.9 who imagined] and imagining *AuW*   99.21 away herevpon] *om. Au1764*   99.30 overtooke and] overtook Us, and *AuW*   99.31 doe] give *AuW*   100.7 lost] left *AuW*   100.19 Soe were you] Sir you was *AuW;* You was *Au1764*   100.23 very greately] at a great Price *AuW*   100.25 I protest] *om. Au1764*   100.27 Andre Uonly] Andrew Honly *AuW;* Andrew Henly *Au1764*   101.20 as abhoring . . . Nature] *om. Au1764*   101.28 some things] some other things *AuW*   102.6 Cattars] *supra;* that which wee call Kitchin Could *s.o.,* E   102.10 sending] being sent *AuW*   103.32 way, which] *AuE ends; AuW becomes copy-text.*   104.14 one of] *AuW orig., but C struck out* one *and added* out. *Au1764 further altered to* out of his Gentleness   108.4 very well] *om. Au1764*   111.14 a great] a greater *Au1764*   112.14 the King] *om. Au1764*   113.22 yet at that] yet come to that *Au1764*   113.35 fed: feed *AuW*

Explanatory Notes

IN THE following notes, references to books included in the Select Bibliography are cited by author and page number. Other works cited:

Alumni Oxoniensis	*Alumni Oxoniensis*, ed. Joseph Foster (1891)
Cal. S.P.	*Calendar of State Papers*, various years
Gardiner, *History*	S. R. Gardiner, *History of England from the Accession of James I to the Outbreak of the Civil War*, 10 vols. (1883–4)
O.E.D.	*Oxford English Dictionary*
Oxford Register	*Register of the University of Oxford*, ed. Andrew Clark (1887)
Walpole's Correspondence	Horace Walpole, *Correspondence*, ed. W. S. Lewis (New Haven, 1937–)
Wheatley and Cunningham	Henry B. Wheatley and Peter Cunningham, *London Past and Present*, 3 vols. (1891)

Page 2. (1) *Lanervil:* modern Llanerfyl in the hundred of Caereinion, Mont.

(2) *forest Bill:* an implement for pruning trees. It has a long blade with a concave edge, often ending in a sharp hook (*O.E.D.*).

(3) *Llyssyn:* near Llanerfyl, Mont.

Page 3. (1) *St. Quintens:* St. Quentin, taken from the French by the English and Spanish on 10 August 1557. The French forces were commanded by Anne, Duc de Montmorenci, Constable of France, whose son and grandson Lord Herbert knew.

(2) *Grand-Fathers power:* His choice of Griffith Lloyd over John Vaughan for sheriff in 1580 probably exacerbated the rivalry between the Herberts and Vaughans to which Lord Herbert refers. (*Cal. S.P., 1577–80*, p. 686).

Page 4. (1) *Black Hall:* also called *Lymore,* was still standing when Lord Herbert retired to it during the Civil War. It was rebuilt after the war,

133

probably by Edward, 3rd Lord Herbert, at which time the Great Hall was 37 ft. by 21 ft. The remains were pulled down about 1930.

(2) *Dolegeog:* modern Dolguog, about $1\frac{1}{4}$ miles from Machynlleth along the Dovey valley.

(3) *Inheretrix:* Jane, heiress of Hugh ap Owen.

(4) *manner:* the canopied tomb of Richard and Magdalen Herbert dominating the south (Lymore) transept of the Montgomery church. Under the canopy lie effigies of Richard Herbert in armour and Magdalen Herbert in an embroidered dress; behind them kneel the figures of eight children. The canopy is ornately decorated with death's heads, fruit, flowers, and the family arms with helm, crest, and mantling.

Page 5. (1) *Hall and Grafton:* Edward Halle, *The Union of Two Noble and Illustrious Families*, 1548 (*STC* 12721), f. ccii.b; Richard Grafton, *A Chronicle at Large, to the first yere of Q. Elizabeth*, 1569 (*STC* 12147).

(2) *Poll-ax:* a kind of battle axe; short-handled weapon hung from the saddle, often with a cutting edge opposite the broad face (*O.E.D.*).

(3) *Knight of the Sun:* a reference to the legendary Amadis de Gall, hero of a prose romance of the same name, supposed to have been written (1508) by Basco de Lobeira, a Portuguese. Amadis de Gall was thought to have been the natural child of Perion, King of Wales, and Elizena, Princess of Brittany.

Page 6. (1) *woollen Beads:* on 2 August 1764 William Cole wrote to Horace Walpole, '*Woolen beads*, I apprehend should be *wooden beads*. Wooden beads are put in contradistinction to any other of more precious materials of metal, stone or jewels, and are commonly used by the poorer people to this day.' (Walpole, *Correspondence*, i. 70.) Although I have found no other references to *woolen* beads, I retain Herbert's version since he found them worth remarking.

(2) *Monument:* a description of the now-ruined monument to Sir Richard Herbert and his wife Margaret appears in Coxe's *Tour in Monmouthshire* (1801), pp. 186–8.

Page 7. (1) *Ragland:* Raglan Castle, Monmouth. Lee says that 'this is a loose statement. The reference is to Elizabeth, daughter of William Herbert (created Earl of Huntingdon 1479), son and heir, and not younger son, of the Earl of Pembroke. She married, about 1490, Charles Somerset, illegitimate son of Henry, Duke of Somerset.'

Page 8. (1) *printed: A Sermon of Commemoration of the Lady Dāuers, late Wife of Sir Iohn Dāuers. Preach'd . . . by Iohn Donne, D. of St. Paul's London, 1. July 1627.* London: 1627. Donne's sermon is printed in G. R. Potter and Evelyn M. Simpson, eds., *The Sermons of John Donne,* VIII. Also see Walton's 'Life of Mr. George Herbert'.

(2) *Berghenapsoom:* modern Bergen-op-Zoom, North Brabant, The Netherlands.

Page 9. (1) *to the East Indias:* the voyage took place in December 1616 when Capt. Benjamin Joseph sailed in the *Globe* as commander. In March 1617 a Portuguese carrack attacked, killing Captain Joseph.

(2) *Company:* an error. Sir Thomas Smith was Governor of the East India Company.

(3) *greate Mogull:* the common designation of the emperor of the Mohammedan Mongol empire in Hindustan. The empire, founded in 1526 by a descendant of Tamerlane, lasted until 1857. Surat was the Mogul's chief port.

(4) *England:* Sir Thomas Roe, first accredited envoy to the Great Mogul, notes in a dispatch from Mandow, 3 November 1617, that 'Mr. Herbert, weary of the progress [of the English merchants toward the court] is bound for England'. He apparently returned to Surat at the end of 1617 and sailed in the *Globe* early the following year. (*Cal. of Colonial Papers, East Indies,* 1617–21.)

(5) *Navy:* Sir Robert Mansell arrived with twenty ships in the roads of Algiers on 27 November 1620 to punish the Dey for his pirating attacks on English ships in the Mediterranean. The fleet was recalled in July 1621. See Gardiner, *History,* iv. 223–5.

Page 10. (1) *to the Lowe Countreys:* Mansfeld, who fought on both sides in the Thirty Years War, returned to Flushing with an English army in January 1624/5. See Gardiner, *History,* v. 285, and *Cambridge Modern History,* iv. 24 ff.

(2) *Seas:* Thomas Herbert was appointed captain of the *Dreadnought* by Buckingham on 25 September 1625. (*Cal. S.P., Dom. 1625–6,* p. 111.)

(3) *Abermarles:* Carmarthenshire, near Llangadock.

Page 11. (1) *Llwydiart:* the marriage took place 3 November 1606 (Montgomery Parish Register).

(2) *Lee:* Peter Legh (*b.* 1623) of Lyme, Lancashire was killed in a duel in London, 1642. See Edward Baines, *History of . . . Lancashire,* James Croston, ed., iv. 388.

(3) *Eyton:* Eyton-on-Severn near Wroxeter, Shropshire. Lord Herbert's birthplace came into the family in 1547 when Sir Thomas Bromley bought it of the crown; it descended to Herbert through his maternal grandmother Newport, Bromley's daughter. Only a tower and a part of a wall now remain.

Page 12. (1) *VITA:* In Smith's edition of Herbert's poetry this poem is entitled 'De Vita Humana Philosophica Disquisitio' and comprises 100 lines. It derives from the 1645 and 1656 editions of *De Causis Errorum.* Both the longer version of 'De Vita Humana' and its companion 'De Vita Celesti' are included in *AuW* and *Au1764*, although Walpole silently altered them. The elliptical conclusion of the version here seems to re-iterate Herbert's known doubts about the validity of one religion to the exclusion of others. The translation printed below will suggest the density of Herbert's Latin verse.

First, life was once contained in a fertile seed where a formative impulse longed to realize its promise, to imbue its shapeless mass with vigorous energy and to keep its outward form in its recess until forces acting to-gether could develop and cause the whole fetus to accustom itself to life in safety. [6]

Next, it grew in its mother's womb where its teeming spirit put on slender, projecting limbs and at the same time wrought the marvellous structure of the senses, creating no mean shelter for the mind, which, gliding down from Heaven, assumed its own functions and, as a sort of indication of future destiny, brought the whole slothful mass into order and made it useful. [13]

The third stage, vast scene, is now disclosed, and revealing the festive theatre of Heaven and Earth, kindred and species, varied forms of things. And it comes to pass that the soul circles and wanders about with its own special movement and perceives the laws and eternal principles of the universe, and the stars revolving in their unending course: from this also can be seen the reasons for life and its obligations. The soul was permitted as well to have a foreknowledge of the greatest divinity from afar, while He harmoniously regulated the varied movements of the Universe and gave easy access to one pouring out holy prayers and supplications. [24]

Thus, the fourth stage follows, when the mind, baseness cast out, now eagerly follows a purer course and there ensues a new hope, conscious of a better fate, clinging to the spiritual things and enlightened by Heaven.

And the Divine Power descends to conjoin holy love; this false token of life is handed over universally; God is not bound by one law alone.

Page 15. (1) *Colledge:* The entry in the *Oxford Register* for 14 May 1596 reads 'Herberte, Edward; Montgom., Arm. f., 14'. The entry in *Alumni Oxoniensis* gives a matriculation date of 'June, 1596'.

(2) *Coma uigilans:* a drowsy sleeplessness sometimes associated with typhus.

(3) *St. Gillians:* St. Julians, Monmouthshire, between Caerleon and Newport.

Page 16. (1) *to Match her:* Philip Herbert, later 4th Earl of Pembroke, was a suitor for her hand in 1597, and Mary 'declared herself to be in love with Philip and vowed she would hear of no other husband'. Despite the support of Philip's father, Mary appears to have broken off the match. See Tresham Lever, *The Herberts of Wilton* (1967), p. 62.

(2) *Vroxeter:* modern Wroxeter, near Shrewsbury. The church contains the family tombs of the Newports.

Page 17. (1) *deboist:* an obsolete form of *debauched* (O.E.D.).

(2) *Chamoepetis: Ckamoedris* [chamaidrys], germander; *chamoepetis* [chemaepitys], ground pine or herb ivy; both medicinal herbs.

(3) *Succoni:* an oil derived from amber.

Page 18. (1) *Comenus:* In Joannes Amos Comenius' *Janua Linguarum* (1631) the equivalents of common phrases in different languages were arranged side by side. The book, frequently published in English, was known as the *Gate of Tongues*; some editions dealt with Latin, Greek, and English phrases, others solely with modern languages. Comenius is not among the authors whose books Herbert bequeathed to Jesus College Library.

Page 19. (1) *accuate:* to sharpen (O.E.D.).

Page 20. (1) *Severnius Danus:* Herbert owned the 1571 (Basel) edition of Severin's *Idea Medicinae Philosophicae.* (Fordyce and Knox, p. 86.)

(2) *contraverted:* Francis Patrizi was well known for his attacks on Aristotle. Herbert owned his *Discussionum peripateticarum* (Basel, 1581). Telesius of Cosenza wrote *De Rerum Natura* (1565; 1586), not included by Fordyce and Knox as among Herbert's bequest.

Page 21. (1) *Succidania:* succedanea; substitutes.

(2) *feaver:* possibly typhus.

Page 22. (1) *Rhue Sayson:* Rhiwsaeson, Llanbrynmair, Montgomery.

(2) *Antidataries:* a collection of antidote recipes; often used synonymously with *dispensary (O.E.D.).*

(3) *Messanensis:* Because Herbert's references in practical medicine are seldom clear, I have listed here the probable titles of the books to which he refers. (a) *Pharmacopoeia Londinensis* (1618), the first pharmacopoeia issued by the Royal College of Physicians; (b) *Codex Medicamentarius seu Pharmacopoeia Parisiensis* (1639), the first Parisian pharmacopoeia; (c) *Pharmacopoea Amstelredamensis. Senatus auctoritate munita & recognita* (1636); (d) Josephus Quercetanus [DuChesne], *Pharmacopoea Dogmaticorum Restituta* (Paris, 1607), by the French champion of Paracelsian medicine; (e) Brice Bauderon's *Pharmacopoea et Praxis Medica* issued in Paris (1620) and London (1639); (f) Joannes Renodaes [Jean de Renou], *Dispensatorium Medicum et Antidotarium* (Paris, 1609); (g) Valerius Cordus's *Pharmacorum omnium* (Nuremburg, 1546), the first genuine pharmacopoeia to be published, recognized as the official pharmacopoeia of Nuremburg. He was also the author of *Annotationes in Pedacii Discoridis Anazarbei de medica materia* (1561), edited by Conrad Gesner (see p. 30, above), which added about 500 plants to Dioscorides's earlier work; (h) either *Dispensarium usuale pro Pharmacopoeis inclytae Reipubl. Colonien* (1565) or the *Pharmacopoea siue Dispensatorium Coloniense* (1627), neither of which is among Herbert's bequest to Jesus College; (i) Herbert was probably referring to the 1613 edition of Adolph Occo's *Enchiridion, sive ut vulgo vocant dispensatorium . . . pharmacopoeis* (Augsburg, 1564), known as *Pharmacopoeia Augustana* (other editions in 1580 and 1622); (j) Lee identifies this reference to Venetiana with Curtio Martinello's *Pharmacopoea a Medicorum Venetorum Collegio Comprobata* (1617)—it may equally refer to the popular *Antidotarium* by Salernitanus Nicolaus (1471); (k) the reference to Vononiensis is almost certainly a scribal error for *Bononiensis*—the *Antidotarium Bononiensis* by U. Aldrovandi was printed in Bologna in 1574 and revised in 1606; (l) two Florentine titles are *Recettario . . . nuovamente mandato in luce* (Venice, 1548) or *Ricettario Fiorentino di nuovo illustrato* (1597; 1623); (m) *Antidotarii Romani, seu de modo compendi medicamenta quae sunt in usu opus* compiled by the Collegium Medicorum with editions in 1583, 1607, 1624; (n) identified by Lee as *Antidotarium Speciale sacrae Domus Magni Hospitalis urbis Messanae* by Placidus Truglio.

Page 23. (1) *Medicorum:* Lee suggested '*Aurora Thesaurusque Philosophorum*

Theoph. Paracelsi, by Paracelsus's pupil Gerard Dorn. Basle 1577, and Frankfort 1585'. Herbert owned Dorn's *Fasciculus Paracelsicae medicinae veteris* (Frankfurt, 1581). See Fordyce and Knox, p. 83.

(2) *Fernelius:* Joannes Fernelius's most famous work was *Universa medicina,* first published in 1578 and as late as 1656. Herbert owned at least three of Fernelius's other works.

(3) *Heurnius:* Herbert owned works by each of the three men he mentions here: Ludovicus Mercatus, Daniel Sennert, and Jan van Heurn. See Fordyce and Knox. pp. 84–6.

(4) *Spagerique:* alchemical. *O.E.D.* cites Herbert's usage.

(5) *Icones:* plates, images.

(6) *Gesnars:* likely Gesner's *Novum dispensatorium* (Venice, 1571),which Herbert owned; he may as well have known Gesner's pocket dictionary of plants, *Historiae plantarum* (Paris, 1541).

Page 24. (1) *Converse:* the ideas expressed in this passage are more fully developed in *De Religione Gentilium* (Amsterdam, 1663), published in London, 1705, under title of *The Antient Religion of the Gentiles,* trans. William Lewis.

Page 25. (1) *emaculate:* to efface.

Page 26. (1) *Punishment on them:* On Herbert's view of forgiveness Walpole added, 'This is a very unchristian reason for pardoning our enemies, and can by no means be properly called Forgiveness. . . . Such sentiments shou'd always be marked and condemned, especially in authors, who certainly do not mean to preach up Malice and Revenge. His Lordship's other reasons are better founded, tho' still selfish. He does not appear a humane philosopher, till he owns that he continued to forgive, tho' he found that it encouraged new Injuries. The beauty of Virtue consists in doing right tho' to one's own prejudice' (p. 40n.).

Page 28. (1) *Quintilian:* Herbert owned several volumes by Cicero and Aristotle (Fordyce and Knox, pp. 77, 79, 92); Quintilian's *Oratoriarum Institutionem* was frequently reprinted during the sixteenth and seventeenth centuries.

Page 31. (1) *the greate horse:* the exceptionally large and powerful war horse which was managed according to fixed rules.

Page 32. (1) *Fleuret:* the modern foil.

Page 33. (1) *rod:* riding whip, crop.

(2) *un pas et un sault:* a pass and turn manoeuvre to gain the advantage. The other terms are also for riding manoeuvres: *Terreterra,* a forward jump; *Courbettes,* leaps in which the forelegs are raised together, equally advanced, and the hind legs raised with a spring before the fore-legs reach the ground; *Cabrioles,* high leaps without advancing.

(3) *Demivolte:* one of the seven artificial motions of a horse; a half turn made with the fore-legs raised.

(4) *Horsemanship:* Salomon de la Broue's *Préceptes principaux* (La Rochelle, 1593–4) was revised and reissued under the new title *Le Cavalerice françois* (Paris, 1602). The British Library owns a copy la Broue presented to James I.

Page 34. (1) *Pluuinel:* Antoine de Pluvinel wrote *L'Instruction du Roy en l'exercice de monter a cheval* (Paris, 1625), of which there were several editions. Menou (see p. 45 below) edited the book in 1640.

Page 36. (1) *Galetaeus:* Giovanni della Casa's *Il Galatheo* (Milan, 1559) was written about 1550 and was a standard educational treatise in Italy for many years. Stefano Guazzo's *La ciuile conuersatione* (Brescia, 1574) appeared in London in 1581 translated by George Pettie and Bartholomew Young.

(2) *Treatise:* This is possibly a reference to what has been generally accepted as Herbert's *Dialogue between a Tutor and a Pupil* (London, 1768); Rossi argues that it is not Herbert's because of serious contradictions between it and his other philosophic treatises (*La Vita,* III, 530–3). For an opposing view see Hutcheson's edition of *De Religio Laici* (1944).

(3) *Leases:* the first of many problems Herbert faced in disposing of family property and income. His high approval of his grandmother in allowing her son Francis Newport complete control of his estates suggests the bitterness Herbert felt when his mother refused to oblige him with a similar trust.

(4) *sister:* Frances, wife of Sir John Brown.

(5) *Essex:* The uprising took place on Sunday, 7 February 1600/1. He was put to death 28 February.

Page 37. (1) *Oath:* Robert Naunton, *Fragmenta Regalia* (1653; reprinted 1870), cites 'God's Death' as the Queen's 'wonted oath' (p. 17).

(2) *Pentioner:* one of the handsome young gentlemen of rank and fortune whom Queen Elizabeth selected for her bodyguards. Cf. *Midsummer Night's Dream,* II. i and *Merry Wives of Windsor,* II. ii.

(3) *Burley:* Burghley House, built in 1560–87 by the great Lord Burghley, is among the most sumptuous of Elizabethan buildings. James I stayed there from Saturday 23 April to Wednesday 27 April 1603.

(4) *Order:* An account of the ceremonial proceedings is published in John Nichols, *The Progresses . . . of King James the First* (1828), ii. 336–41.

Page 38. (1) *study:* The large full-length portrait, artist unknown, now hangs in Powis Castle, Welshpool, the seat of the Earl of Powis.

(2) *handsommest:* The lady to whom Herbert alludes here and on p. 60 below cannot be identified with certainty. John Selden said that 'Lady Kent articled with Sir *Edward Herbert* that he should come to her when she sent for him and stay with her as long as she would have him, to which he set his hand; then he articled with her, that he should go away when he pleas'd, and stay away as long as he pleas'd, to which she set her hand'. (*Table Talk*, ed. Arber, 1868, p. 41.) D. A. Keister, 'Lady Kent and the Two Sir Edwards', *Modern Language Notes,* lxi (1956), 169–72, argues convincingly that Selden was referring to Sir Edward, the attorney-general. The woman to whom Selden referred was probably Elizabeth Talbot, wife of Henry, 6th Earl of Kent.

(3) *to Spaine:* February 1604/5. See Ralph Winwood's *Memorials* (1725), II, 50.

Page 39. (1) *Herbert:* Edward resigned his pretence to Montgomery Castle in 1606 after his distant kinsman Philip Herbert, brother to the 3rd Earl of Pembroke, was created Earl of Montgomery. Herbert regained possession of the castle in 1613 when he paid £500, but in 1616 it was granted to the Sir William he mentions here to administer for the Crown, although Herbert once again soon regained possession. (See *Montgomeryshire Collections*, x. 168ff.)

(2) *Dutton:* probably the Mr. Detton whose name appears frequently in Magdalen Herbert's *Kitchin Book* and in the letters of Sir John Danvers to Edward Herbert. (See *La Vita*, i. 49, 77; iii. 402–3.) Lee makes no mention of Dutton because the passage was missing from his copy-text.

Page 40. (1) *Cradle:* apparently a proverbial reference. See John Ray, *English Proverbs*, 'Cast not thy cradle over thy head', dated 1678.

Page 41. (1) *St. Germains:* In his 'Satyra Secunda' subtitled 'Of Travellers: (from Paris)' Herbert writes to Ben Jonson of Englishmen in Paris that:

> . . . all they learn is
> Toyes, and the Language: but to attain this,

> You must conceive, they'r cousen'd, mock'd & come
> To *Fauxbourgs St. Germans*, there take a Room
> Lightly about th' Ambassadors, and where,
> Having no Church, they come *Sundays*, to hear,
> An invitation. . . . (ll. 22–8)

Page 42. (1) *Merlou:* The village of Mello near Clermont (Oise) is about 30 miles north of Paris. Herbert's sonnet 'Made upon the Groves near Merlow Castle' indicates the delight he took in the beauty of the castle's surroundings.

(2) *Reband:* ribbon.

Page 43. (1) *Uaughan:* unidentified; another incident in the long rivalry between the Herberts and the Vaughans.

(2) *Vanachly:* I have been unable to identify James Price with certainty, although he was probably a descendant of Mathew Price, Herbert's great-grandfather.

Page 44. (1) *Gentleman:* John Chamberlain wrote to Dudley Carleton on 23 January 1610 of a quarrel between 'Sir Edw. Herbert and Boqhuan [Buchan?], a Scotch Gentleman, Usher of the Queen, about a ribbon taken from Mrs. Middlemore'. (*Cal. S.P., Dom.,* viii. 583.)

Page 45. (1) *Chantilly:* The Chateau built for Anne de Montmorenci about 1560, now occupied by the Musée Condé, stands on the east edge of the town near the forest of Chantilly.

(2) *Mennon:* Probably a reference to René de Menou, friend of Pluvinel and editor of his book, *La Manège Royale.*

Page 47. (1) *founded:* endowed; a rare usage.

Page 49. (1) *did litle: AuW*'s emendation, 'did not a litle', makes this ambiguous passage clear.

(2) *Margaret:* Marguerite of Valois. Her marriage to Henri of Navarre was dissolved at his accession as Henri IV, although she remained on good terms with him and Marie de Medici and bore the title of queen. In his second satire Herbert writes of 'the little fry'

> That all along the street turn up the eye
> At every thing they meet, that have not yet
> Seen that swoln vitious Queen, *Margaret,*
> Who were a monster ev'n without her sin. (ll. 82–6)

Page 50. (1) *January:* 1609.

Page 52. (1) *ipse:* This portrait is now lost, although a print of it was published in 1768. (See *La Vita,* iii. 385–9, for a survey of the seven known portraits of Herbert.) Edmund Blunden translates the motto as: Make me, Almighty Goodness, wholly good; Myself, I'll answer for my hardihood. (*Votive Tablets,* 1931, p. 54.)

(2) *War:* The war broke out over the disputed succession to the duchy of Cleves resulting from the death of William John, Duke of Cleves, in March 1609. Two claimants, the Elector of Brandenburg and the Palatine of Newbourg, seized the duchy on behalf of the Protestant princes of the Empire. The Emperor Rudolf II of the Austrian Habsburgs then commanded Archduke Leopold to occupy the duchy in his name. After Leopold gained Juliers (Jülich), Henri IV of France announced his support of the two Protestant princes in opposition to the Habsburg rule; England and Holland pledged their assistance. The Spanish, opposing a Protestant state near their territory, sided with the Emperor. Although Henri was assassinated in May, 1610, the Queen after some hesitation ordered Marshal de la Châtre to march against Juliers. The English and the Dutch forces began the siege on 17 July and many of the mines were well underway by the time the French forces arrived on 8 August. Juliers surrendered on 22 August 1610.

Page 53. (1) *Sentinells Perdues:* advanced sentries.

Page 54. (1) *Cortine:* in fortification that part of the wall which connects two bastions or towers.

(2) *charge again:* this refers to reloading their weapons, not to an attack by foot or cavalry.

(3) *Crosse:* as Lee first realized, the *Crofts* which had been printed in all editions before his was an error; no one by that name had written about the siege of Juliers. In 1627 William Crosse published a second edition and continuation of Edward Grimestone's *Generall Historie of the Netherlands* (1608). Crosse writes, 'The English sapped or mined first into the wall before *Chatillion* or *Bethun* had advanced so farre; the truth whereof Sir *Edward Harbert,* now Lord *Harbert* of Castle Island, can approue; who carried himselfe most valiantly in all that Service, and brought away a mark of Honour, as beeing the first of all the Nations then passed ouer into the wall. This I speake not out of any nationall partialitie'. He adds marginally, 'Gentle reader, if you chance to see any copie with any other name

than that of Sir *Edw. Herbert* here specified, know it was mistaken in the printing' (p. 1294).

(4) *Quarrel:* The quarrel is narrated more fully in Lansdowne MS. XCIX, an account by Lord Howard's second, Sir Thomas Peyton. According to Peyton, Sir Edward Cecil quickly intervened and effected a reconciliation which Herbert violated by issuing a new challenge four or five days later. Herbert then failed to appear at the appointed place. As Rossi points out (*La Vita,* iii. 382–5), Peyton's narration is unreliable both in time and fact; Lee, who printed it as Appendix V to his edition, wilfully altered the MS. to make Herbert appear in the worst possible light. An additional reference to the quarrel occurs in Winwood's letter to the Earl of Salisbury, 22 August 1610: 'Sir *Edward Herbert* (will they nill they) hath forced a Quarrel since my coming from the Army, first upon my Lord *Walden,* after upon Sir *Thomas Somersett,* your Lordship may understand by these Gentlemen, [in a postscript] who then were present: Wherein he hath offered an irreparable Injurie to my Lord Generall, who hath treated him, as he hath done them all, with an exceeding Love and kindness' (*Memorials,* iii. 210).

Page 55. (1) *Areskins:* Although the name was written as *Erskins* in the Peyton account of the quarrel, which he presumably examined, Lee says, 'Probably a misreading for Erskine'. For once, however, the scribe's erratic spelling has a confirmation. The *Alphabeticel register . . . Commissien 1600–1640* (Rijks-Archeif, The Hague) shows that 'James Arskine' was appointed 'Capitain' in 1617 (f. 2ᵛ).

Page 57. (1) *Paillard:* lecherous or lewd person.

Page 58. (1) *surrendered:* 22 August 1610.

Page 60. (1) *Dorset House:* on Fleet Street. Formerly the possession of the Bishops of Salisbury, it was destroyed in the Great Fire of 1666 and never rebuilt. (Wheatley and Cunningham, i. 515.)

(2) *Picture:* At Charlecote Park, now part of the National Trust, the Lucy family owned a portrait painted on copper which seems to be the one presented to Sir Thomas Lucy.

(3) *greater person:* Lee identifies her as 'probably Queen Anne', but Rossi discounts the possibility that her interest was more than momentary. (*La Vita,* i. 168–9.) In his letter of 5 October 1764 George Montagu wrote to Horace Walpole about the frontispiece of the 1764 edition that he

'never saw so charming a figure so well graved, so sweet a romantic landscape—all Tasso, all Spencer, all truth, all honest, all spirit, that I wonder not old Bess patted his cheeks. What Ann of Denmark patted he does not tell yet'. (Walpole's *Correspondence*, x. 133-4.)

Page 61. (1) *Person:* possibly Queen Anne.

Page 64. (1) *Humfrey Uill:* Previous editions have printed *Humphrey Hill* here. I suspect (but have no evidence) that Herbert was referring to one of the Umfreville family.

Page 66. (1) *letter:* The letter from Montmorenci is now lost.

Page 67. (1) *Husk:* the river Usk which flows SW of the town.
   (2) *Colebrook:* Coldbrook, near Abergavenny, Monmouthshire.

Page 72. (1) *Peace:* Together with the French ambassador, Wotton arranged a temporary peace at Xanten on 2 November 1614. Neither Spinola nor Prince Maurice accepted the terms and the war was renewed the following year. (See L. P. Smith, *Life and Letters of Sir Henry Wotton*, 1907, ii. 41-59.)
   (2) *Kysarswert:* Kaiserswerth near Düsseldorf.
   (3) *St. Herbert:* The monastery Herbert saw was a Benedictine abbey founded by St. Heribert in 1003 on the east bank of the Rhine in what is now the suburb of Deutz. Heribert had been made archbishop of Cologne in 999 by his patron Emperor Otto III.

Page 73. (1) *Augsbourg:* No German archives exist to substantiate Herbert's account. On 26 January 1614/15 Herbert's agent Richard Prytherugh (Prothero) wrote that he had received Herbert's letter from 'Augsburgh'. (Smith, *Correspondence*, p. 69.) Sir John Danvers wrote to Herbert on 26 November 1614 assuring him that his debt of £20 incurred at Augsburg would be discharged.
   (2) *prevented:* preceded or anticipated.
   (3) *Colledge:* Herbert's name does not appear in the *Book of Pilgrims*, vol. VI of *Records of the English Province of the Society of Jesus* (1880). Although many obvious English pseudonyms appear, it seems unlikely that Herbert would have registered at all since he was neither a pilgrim nor a guest in the hospice.

Page 75. (1) *his Excellency:* Count Maurice of Nassau.

Page 76. (1) *Navarra:* Novara.
   (2) *Ollas podridas:* Spanish *olla podrida*, rotten pot; a dish composed of

pieces of many kinds of meat, vegetables, and spices stewed or boiled together.

(3) *Comfett:* a comfit; a sweetmeat of fruit preserved with sugar, or a small round mass of sugar enclosing a caraway seed.

(4) *Mount Cenis:* Italian, *Moncenisio*; an alpine pass (6,831 ft.) between France and Italy on the direct route from Turin to Lyon.

(5) *Scarnafigi:* When the Spaniards ignored the treaty of Asti which had temporarily ended hostilities between Savoy and Spain, Count Scarnafissi was dispatched to England to seek aid for Charles Emanuel. Ralegh, then imprisoned, proposed a diversionary attack on Genoa, but the proposal was never carried out. See Gardiner, *History*, iii. 49–52.

Page 77. (1) *warr:* against the Spanish.

Page 78. (1) *Pole:* poll; head.
(2) *Forme:* a bench.

Page 79. (1) *Gabelet:* Despite the assistance of the staff of the British Museum map room this reference remains unidentified.
(2) *Burgoin:* about 25 miles SE of Lyon.
(3) *Nackarine:* red, reddish. Lord Herbert's is the only use of this rare word listed in *O.E.D.*

Page 80. (1) *Mother:* Marie de Medici (1573–1642), daughter of Francis de' Medici, married Henri IV of France in October 1600 after his marriage with Marguerite of Valois was dissolved. After his assassination in 1610 she tried with some success to control the fractious princes, her fortunes improving when Richelieu came to influence in 1616. Imprisoned by her son, Louis XIII, she escaped in 1619 and became the centre of a revolt but they were later reconciled. For the last twenty years of her life she intrigued with little success against Richelieu.

Page 85. (1) *Elector:* Four letters from the Elector and Elizabeth are among the Powis papers in the Public Records Office.
(2) *St. Islands:* Sandilands.
(3) *Reswick:* Rijswijk, two miles SE of the Hague, where the House of Orange had a castle.

Page 86. (1) *Asti:* in the Piedmont, thirty miles SE of Turin.
(2) *Brill:* or Brielle is 13 miles W of Rotterdam on the mouth of the Brielsche Maas. English garrisons in Flushing and Brill were concessions

by the States General in return for the aid of an auxiliary army under the Earl of Leicester (1585).

Page 87. (1) *Graveling:* Gravelines, 12 miles from Dunkirk.

Page 89. (1) *old Exchange:* named from the King's Exchange which was used to store bullion, it has been called Old Change since the early seventeenth century. The street runs from Cheapside to Knightrider Street.

(2) *Alliance:* concluded 19 August 1610 during the minority of Louis XIII. Lord Herbert's instructions were general in nature, urging the maintenance of peaceful relations between the two countries. His instructions are printed in *Montgomeryshire Collections*, vi. 417–19.

Page 90. (1) *Uaughan:* probably one of the Vaughan family with whom the Herberts had long been at odds, especially over the inheritance of John Vaughan, husband of Herbert's sister Margaret. See p. 11 above and *La Vita*, ii. 16–17.

Page 91. (1) *Burial:* Queen Anne's burial took place after many delays on 13 May 1619, although she had died on 18 March. Sir Gerard Herbert wrote to Sir Dudley Carleton on 19 March that 'Sir Edward Herbert is going to France and his brother Harry is gone to prepare for him'. (*Cal. S.P.* Dom., 1619–23, p. 25.)

(2) *Tallemant and Rambouillet:* another firm of bankers with whom Herbert and his predecessors had dealings. By the beginning of June 1621 Herbert owed the firm 30,353.13.4 *livres tournois* (about £3,050). Public Records Office, 30/53, formerly Powis MS. II, IV, 190.

Page 92. (1) *Memmon:* probably René de Menou; see p. 45 above.

Page 94. (1) *War:* In 1619 the supporters of the Queen-mother released her from Blois and secured some concessions for her by the peace of Angoulême. When her followers attempted to override the treaty the next year an army under Louis XIII defeated them.

Page 95. (1) *London:* Six volumes of Herbert's letters and dispatches from his embassy in France are now in the Public Records Office (class 30/53), but the volume to which he may have devoted some time is Add. MS. 7082, *Sir Edw. Herbert's Book of Despatches in 1619*, which includes his original letter of appointment dated from Theobalds, 9 May 1619, together with the significant letters of the year.

(2) *Prague:* The battle of Prague, also known as the battle of White

Mountain, 29 October 1620, was an early and decisive battle of the Thirty Years War in which the Protestant forces lost with hardly a shot being fired. Frederick, the Elector Palatine, and his wife Elizabeth were forced into distressful circumstances.

(3) *Crofts:* not identified. Lee supposes him a relative of the Sir James and Sir Herbert Croft already mentioned.

Page 96. (1) *Oliver Herbert:* Perhaps descended from Herbert's grand-uncle, Oliver Herbert of Machynlleth; probably the Oliver who was present at Montgomery Castle during the siege in October 1644. (See *La Vita,* i. 12.)

Page 97. (1) *booke:* no copy is known.

Page 100. (1) *Pundonores:* a contraction of *punto de honor,* point of honour.

(2) *Manuscript:* Lesdiguères' *Discours de l'art Militaire* was printed from a manuscript in the Grenoble library in *Actes et Correspondences du Connétable de Lesdiguères,* ii (1878). The manuscript to which Herbert refers is now lost.

(3) *Uonly:* in previous editions printed as *Henly.* Although 148 foreign tailors are listed in Cooper's *Lists of Foreign Protestants* (Camden Society, lxxxii, 1862), none by either name appears.

Page 101. (1) *Knight:* Although he mentions him only once here, Herbert seems to have enjoyed a cordial relationship with his step-father and contemporary. Aubrey, to whom Danvers was distantly related, has an account of Danvers's later marriage.

Page 103. (1) *Queene:* Anne of Austria.

Page 104. (1) *Martial Persons:* Herbert wrote to Secretary Naunton on 23 March 1622/3 that Louis XIII first proposed the use of force (Lee).

Page 107. (1) *Arnaud:* Perhaps one of the sons of Anthoine de la Mothe-Arnauld.

Page 110. (1) *repeal'd:* Lord Herbert's memory is at fault here. The Marquis de Cadenet, Luynes's brother, visited England in January 1621 before Herbert's break with Luynes occurred. De Cadenet returned to France early in 1621 after his unsuccessful attempt to negotiate an alliance. See Gardiner, *History,* iii. 389, and Rossi, *La Vita,* ii. 189–200.

(2) *Train:* Rémusat says that Du Moulin came to England to make complaint against Lord Herbert in the summer of 1621 (*La Vie de Lord Herbert,* p. 83). Rossi suggests that Du Moulin had other reasons for coming

to England and points out that the story is confused and probably incapable of complete explanation (*La Vita*, ii. 174–80).

(3) *Combate:* Roger Coke's *Detection of the Court and State of England*, i (1694), offers independent confirmation of Herbert's account. Coke relates that after the Earl of Carlisle reported the truth to the King, Herbert 'kneeled to the King' and sought to send a challenge to Luynes for his 'false Relation' to the King; the request was refused (p. 113).

(4) *death:* 21 December 1621.

(5) *France:* James Hay, Earl of Carlisle, had lived in France in his youth and had been ambassador there in 1616.

Page 112. (1) *Valentina:* The Valtellina in northern Italy is the broad valley of the river Adda, occupied by the Swiss confederates from 1512 until 1797.

Page 117. (1) *Sister:* Maria, wife of Philip IV of Spain.

Page 120. (1) *finished: De veritate prout distinguitur à revelatione verisimili, possibili, et à falso* (Paris, 1624, 1636). A French translation was published in 1639. The first London edition appeared in 1633; the second in 1639. The original MS. is now in the British Library, Sloane MS. A 3957.

(2) *scholar:* The relationship between Grotius and Herbert still awaits exploration, but some facts are known. Herbert knew Grotius in Paris during both his first and second embassies. In a letter to J. van Reigersberch, 16 July 1621, Grotius substantiates Herbert's support of the Protestants. When Grotius completed his famous *De jure belli et pacis* in 1624 he presented Herbert a copy, but the one Herbert bequeathed to Jesus College is the 1642 edition. Herbert's poem 'De Hugone Grotio' and the letters among the Powis manuscripts (now Public Record Office) indicate the familiarity Herbert and Grotius shared. (For assistance in translating the Dutch letters of Hugo Grotius I thank Mr. Anthony VanderSchaaf.)

Page 121. (1) *France:* James Hay, Earl of Carlisle, and Henry Rich, later Earl of Holland, arrived in Paris to negotiate the marriage between Henrietta Maria and Prince Charles. Herbert returned to England 24 July 1624 with hopes of becoming vice-chamberlain. (Chamberlain to Carleton, 24 July 1624, *Cal. S.P.* Dom.) Herbert's letter of recall was dated 14/24 April 1624 but, as Conway wrote to Herbert, the early notification was 'to giue your Lordship the most tyme I can for your owne preparation'. (*State Papers*, P.R.O. 78/72, 168–9.)

Index of Persons and Places

'EH' indicates Lord Herbert; family identifications show relationship to him.